Borderline Personality Disorder:

A PATIENT'S GUIDE TO TAKING CONTROL

Borderline Personality Disorder:

A PATIENT'S GUIDE TO TAKING CONTROL

Gina M. Fusco

Arthur Freeman

 W. W. NORTON & COMPANY · NEW YORK · LONDON

W. W. Norton & Company has been independent since its founding in 1923, when William Warder Norton and Mary D. Herter Norton first published lectures delivered at the People's Institute, the adult education division of New York City's Cooper Union. The Nortons soon expanded their program beyond the Institute, publishing books by celebrated academics from America and abroad. By mid-century, the two major pillars of Norton's publishing program—trade books and college texts—were firmly established. In the 1950s, the Norton family transferred control of the company to its employees, and today—with a staff of four hundred and a comparable number of trade, college, and professional titles published each year—W. W. Norton & Company stands as the largest and oldest publishing house owned wholly by its employees.

The text of this book is composed in Palatino with the display set in Optima
Manufacturing by Victor Graphics, Inc.
Production manager: Ben Reynolds
Book design by Julia Druskin
Page makeup by Carole Desnoes

Library of Congress Cataloging-in-Publication Data

Fusco, Gina M.
Borderline personality disorder : a patients's guide to taking control / Gina M. Fusco, Arthur Freeman.
p. cm.
"A Norton professional book."
ISBN 0-393-70353-3 (pbk.)
1. Borderline personality disorder—Popular works. I. Freeman, Arthur, 1942–. II. Title.
RC569.5.B67F874 2003
616.85'852—dc21   2003041326

W. W. Norton & Company, Inc., 500 Fifth Avenue, New York, NY 10110
www.wwnorton.com

W. W. Norton & Company Ltd., Castle House, 75/76 Wells St., London W1T 3QT
1 2 3 4 5 6 7 8 9 0

Contents

Acknowledgments

A project of this magnitude has many roots. First and foremost are our teachers and mentors who have over the years helped us develop insight, skills, empathy, and understanding.

Second are our patients who have entrusted us with their wellbeing and have taught us much about the human condition. It is to them that we have dedicated our professional careers.

Third have been our students who have asked the questions that have stimulated and driven our need to develop programs and protocols for treating the broad range of emotional and behavioral disorders.

Fourth are our colleagues, especially at Philadelphia College of Osteopathic Medicine who have served as sounding boards for our ideas. The support staff, especially Susan Hartman, have typed, copied, collated, and organized the various iterations of these manuscripts. Additional thanks are also due to Alternative Behavioral Services, a comprehensive behavioral healthcare program for high-risk adolescents, that provided Gina M. Fusco with flexibility and support for this and other projects.

Fifth is the staff at W.W. Norton, especially Michael McGandy, Deborah Malmud, and Casey Ruble who have given us the chance to share our ideas with you the reader. They have also given shape and clarity to our presentation.

Finally, we want to thank our families. Arthur Freeman would like to thank his wife, partner, and colleague, Dr. Sharon Freeman for her continuing support, ideas, and love. He would also like to dedicate these volumes to their children: Andrew, Russell, April, Laura, Aaron, Heather, and Rebecca. Gina M. Fusco would like to thank her family, especially her mother Jeanette, and her sisters Cynthia, Elizabeth, and Holly. They have and continue to provide the inspiration and guidance needed to continue this work. Additionally, she would like to thank Stephanie Widder and Marni Nutkowitz, who through their friendship, have provided much laughter, support, and encouragement.

Borderline Personality Disorder:

A PATIENT'S GUIDE TO TAKING CONTROL

Introduction:
Borderline Personality Disorder
& Understanding the
Development of Schemas

Perhaps at one time you felt or were told that you are depressed or maybe that you are the "anxious type." Being down in the dumps, having little to no energy, feeling sad, and having problems concentrating are some of the symptoms associated with depression. If you've been anxious, you recognize that sinking feeling in your stomach, racing heart, and sweaty palms. Depression and anxiety are mental disorders that are easily identified and understood. But what is borderline personality disorder (BPD)? And how do you know if it is something you have? If you do have it, is there a "cure" for it?

Clinicians have been asked these very questions by patients seeking to understand why they react in certain ways and why they have certain behavioral patterns. Or why they feel as if they are never really able to feel "settled" in their own skin. These are important and relevant questions.

YOUR PERSONALITY

To begin with, we may ask: What is a personality? Philosophers throughout the ages have asked that very question. Are we created in the image of a greater being, or are we a collection of drives that stem from our biology? Do we carry certain traits from our families and learn to do what they do? In other words, have we inherited what we are to become, or do we learn it? Generally, psychology views personality as a set of inherited tendencies or predispositions that act in conjunction with our environment. In this way, we can understand that our personalities are influenced by our genes but not completely determined by them. Depending on our environment, our genetic predispositions may or may not be expressed. The important thing to understand is that our personalities are not set in stone; we have choices and options.

A personality is what we generally think of as who we are. It is the set of characteristics that is unique to us, the consistent parts of ourselves that tend to react and respond in the same ways. Our characteristics usually can be traced from early childhood through adolescence and into adulthood. They include how we uniquely think, feel, react, and handle situations. For example, if you were somewhat shy in your high school years, you may as an adult still struggle or feel uncomfortable when you are around a large group of people. Our personality also is our predominant traits, expectations, and beliefs.

Let's take a moment to see if you can identify some of your features or traits. Would you say, for example, that you are outgoing, shy, moody, or highly emotional? List five:

3

1. _____

   _____ .

2. _____

   _____ .

3. _____

   _____ .

4. _____

   _____ .

5. _____

   _____ .

How did you do? What were the characteristics that you noted about yourself? It is important to understand that personality is a set of patterns—a set of patterned behaviors, feelings, thoughts, perceptions, and physiological reactions that combine to create you.

So what makes someone have a personality disorder? A personality disorder is defined as "an enduring pattern of inner experience and behavior that deviates from the expectations of the individual's culture, is pervasive and inflexible, has an onset in adolescence or early adulthood, is stable over time, and leads to distress or impairment" (APA, 2000, p. 685). So what does that mean? A personality disorder has a few components. First, it is a pattern of how you see and perceive yourself, and how your behaviors are expressed outwardly. However, these behaviors and experiences *deviate,* or are different from, those of others in your culture. *Culture* means those who are similar to you by virtue of age, background, family, or ethnicity. A personality disorder is also *pervasive and inflexible.* This means that the way you view yourself and project yourself tends to remain the same over time and across situations. Most people tend to react to things in a fixed and predictable way. Again, personality characteristics usually are established by early adulthood or adolescence. People who have personality disorders experience intense distress or upset, and may often have problems functioning. This could occur in their work setting, within relationships, or with respect to how they feel about or view themselves.

If we put the pieces together, we see that *personality* has to do with your unique and stable way of viewing yourself, your world, and your interactions with the world. It includes behaviors, feelings, thoughts, and interactions with and reactions toward other people that tend to occur in the same way across time. In particular, those with BPD experience a pattern of instability in interpersonal relationships, self-image, and moods; they tend to be impulsive. The idea of a *cure* implies the removal of detrimental effects on the organism or being. People with personality disorders cannot be cured in the traditional sense. Rather they learn to understand themselves and alter the patterns with which they are unhappy.

HOW DO YOU KNOW IF YOU HAVE BPD?

If you have not found this manual through the recommendation of a licensed clinician or therapist, we suggest that you seek professional consultation in order to determine whether or not you have BPD general psychological principles covered within this manual are referenced in the Therapist Manual. Keep in mind, *everyone experiences varying levels of some of the symptoms of this disorder*. This makes it difficult to ascertain whether the disorder is present and, if it is present, the degree of severity.

Checklist of BPD Symptoms

The following checklist will help you determine if you have had or are experiencing symptoms of BPD. Some of the symptoms may never have occurred for you. Other symptoms may have occurred for you in the past but no longer appear in your current life situation. However, as you answer the following questions, keep in mind your general personality or personality patterns.

1. Do you have a general pattern of instability throughout your life?

2. Do you tend to feel frightened, even terrified, of having others leave you?

3. Do your relationships tend to be intense and unstable, with your view of others switching between being all good and all bad?

4. Do you often feel as if you don't know yourself or are unsure about who you really are?

5. Do you tend to be impulsive? Do you do things without thinking first?

6. Do you ever have suicidal thoughts or thoughts of harming or mutilating yourself?

7. Do you consider yourself to be moody?

8. Do you often feel empty inside?

9. Do you have trouble controlling your anger?

10. Have you experienced either feeling suspicious of others or feeling "outside" of yourself, as if you were watching yourself on a movie screen?

(Adapted from *DSM-IV-TR* [APA, 2000])

If you answered "yes" to five or more of the questions, you may have a borderline personality pattern. This is not an absolute determination, however. If you find you have difficulty in four of the areas, you may still benefit from this workbook. *Again, this is not a means of diagnosing yourself*, but rather a way to determine if this manual will be helpful for you.

The following is a case example of a 27-year-old woman who demonstrates a borderline personality pattern. The underlying theme of her personality is one of instability in all areas of her life. Are there aspects of her character that are similar to your own?

Case Example

Tracey was a 27-year-old, single woman who lived in an apartment in the city. She was the second child of a family of three children. Her parents divorced when Tracey was 13, and she still remembered their divorce as a very painful time in her life. She kept in touch with her parents, who lived in the suburbs, but their relationship was often strained. Tracey worked in sales at a local cell phone company. She enjoyed her job but tended to get bored very easily. She had changed jobs frequently in an attempt to figure out which job would really "fit" her personality.

Tracey described herself as having difficulty with her moods and said that, when she least expected it, she had feelings of sadness that seemed to overwhelm her. The mood changes usually were short in duration, but they affected her social and personal relationships. Sometimes her mood became so low that she considered what it would be like if she were no longer living. She hadn't actually tried to hurt or kill herself, but she tended to become very morbid when she felt down. When she was younger she scratched her arms with sharp objects when she was sad, but she hadn't done that in a long time. Tracey described herself as incredibly sensitive and easily upset by others. Her mother used to tell her she needed "tougher skin" or she would "never make it in life." She just always seemed to take things more deeply and seriously than others, and she found it hard to "shake things off." She also recalled that when she was very stressed, low, or angry she lost track of time and almost felt outside of herself.

Tracey had difficulty understanding why her relationships with men usually didn't last. She tended to rush in to relationships, quickly becoming trusting and intimate (both emotionally and physically) with the person. She also became insecure in the relationship very quickly. She tended to want frequent contact with the man she was dating, and usually called him several times a day, dropped by, or asked to see him more frequently than he desired. Some men even told her that she was "clingy" and that they needed more "space" in the relationship.

Tracey usually regreted her impulsive behaviors but couldn't resist them. At times she drank alcohol until she passed out and couldn't remember getting home. Some nights she even tried a new drug her friends were using. She tended to say things impulsively when she was angry, which caused several breaks in friendships. She couldn't understand why she so easily changed the way she looked at people. Sometimes she felt like those around her understood her perfectly and couldn't do anything wrong; other times she thought they were insensitive, uncaring, and not deserving of her time or her friendship. These intense fluctuations with others caused her much confusion and prevented long-standing relationships from developing. She found that she had to make new friends frequently.

Probably one of the most difficult aspects of Tracey's life had to do with her feelings about herself. She often felt very down about herself, questioned who and what she wanted, and lost direction easily. At times she felt so empty inside that she sought out others to help her fill the gap. The emptiness was especially bad when she wasn't busy working or hanging out with her friends. Tracey couldn't understand this emptiness, but knew that it hurt like a dull ache inside. She often questioned her own identity and looked to others to help define herself. On some occasions she was the witty young woman who was fun, quick to please, and exciting. On other occasions, she seemed to become the needy, dependent person who wanted someone to care for her. She also became very angry if others didn't meet those needs. It became very confusing for her and, similarly, her sudden changes in mood confused those around her.

Overall, Tracey was trying to understand herself, but had much difficulty doing so. Her instability in how she viewed others and herself, as well as her lack of direction, often prevented her from establishing concrete goals. Her sadness at times seemed overwhelming. She described herself as very sensitive and as having intense feelings of emptiness that made her feel vulnerable, without direction, and without purpose. Generally, Tracey was able to function every day by going to work, but she felt as if there was no "homebase" within herself. She seemed to lack a sense of a solid ground she could rely upon. She didn't know how she came to be this way. Tracey wished she could find that solid, predictable part within herself, but she didn't know how to do so.

SCHEMAS

We have all learned about rules. We have learned about them at home, in school, at our place of worship, and on the job. We have learned that we can avoid certain rules, bend some, and even break others. Sometimes there is a price for breaking the rules, sometimes we get away with it, and sometimes the rules are so powerful that they cannot be broken. In every action, reaction, and interaction we are guided by the personal, cultural, religious, beliefs or rules. These rules are often refined and specified by one's age, gender, and/or place in the family. They do not suddenly occur but rather have developed over the years. These ideas or beliefs have been given many different names. They are called *rules of life*, *life attitudes*, *basic beliefs*, *core beliefs*, or *schemas*. The term that we are going to use in this program to discuss the rules that each of us live by is the last of the list; *schemas* (Beck & Emery, 1979).

Our schemas are important because they direct our behavior and emotions, and they thereby help give meaning to our world. The extent and manner of our responses to life situations and our perceptions of situations and other people are functions of how powerful these beliefs are, how much we believe them, how important they are to us, how old we were when we learned them, and from whom they were learned. Our schemas are involved in every aspect of our thinking. They are involved in memory (e.g., what we choose to recall or what is "suppressed"), in cognitive processes (e.g., the collection and interpretation of information), in emotion (e.g., the generation of our feelings), in motivation (e.g., our wishes and desires), and in action and control (e.g., the self-monitoring, inhibition, or direction of action). In fact, the jobs and

careers we choose, the partners to whom we are attracted, and the hobbies in which we engage ourselves are similarly governed by our schemas.

A great example of how schemas affect our lives can be found in the story of the famous open ocean racer, Sir Francis Chichester.

> Chicester was known for his single-handed transoceanic crossings in very small boats. He would race across the Atlantic Ocean, and would sometimes be alone for several weeks at a time. Although married with children, he loved being alone. He was best known for having crossed the Atlantic in a 17-foot boat, *The Gypsy Moth*. After this incredible voyage, he was interviewed and was quoted as saying, "Somehow, I never seemed to enjoy so much doing things with other people. I know I don't do a thing nearly so well when with someone. It makes me think I was cut out for solo jobs, and any attempt to diverge from that lot only makes me half a person." Chichester described himself as a very autonomous and independent individual. Not many of us would be willing to take such risks or be alone for 65 days on a boat in the middle of the ocean. Many of us would see that as akin to solitary confinement. Yet because his life was governed by these independence schemas, Chichester sought a career that allowed him the maximum expression of those schemas.

The following sections cover the formation and function of schemas and how they affect your life. Later, you will have a chance to identify your own rules or schemas, and begin to determine what effect they have on your life. This will help you understand your behavior and your participation in your roles as a member of your family, social group, and work environment.

Your schemas are the wellspring for the perceptions that generate your behavior.

Where Do Schemas Come From?

Schemas and the thoughts, feelings, and behaviors that result from them began to be established from the moment you were born. Today, you hold onto some of these schemas very strongly, while others are more transient and easily surrendered. For example, many people would be reluctant to eat worms or the meat of a dog. This is because mainstream American culture believes that only certain meats are edible and dog and worms are not in that group. The accompanying schema is another that states "One should only have to eat edible meats." If, however, you were in a situation where only dogs or worms were available, the schema that "I must do everything that I can to survive" might become more prominent. Thus, until other foods were available, you would eat (and maybe even relish) a burger made of dog or worms.

The schemas that you hold most strongly become the ways in which you define yourself and how you are defined by others. A particular pattern of schemas about the need for perfection in all of your thoughts and deeds would probably result in your seeing the world in dichotomous terms such as black/white, good/bad, or right/wrong. This would make you demand perfect performance from yourself and others, and probably make you feel that a 98% success rate constituted a failure.

Schemas are not isolated but, rather, are interlocking and appear in various combinations. For example, while most of us would subscribe to the basic personal/religious/cultural schema "Thou shalt not steal," if a pay phone accidentally returned our quarter after we completed a call, we probably would not return money to the phone company. Our rationale for this would be based on other schemas such as "Getting even is okay or important," which may serve to generate the idea that "Because the phone company has taken our money for so many years we can rightfully take their's."

If, however, we apply the rule "Getting even is okay or important" more broadly, it would allow us to take money from someone else (stranger or friend) even if our money had been taken by another, unrelated person. If we apply the rule "Getting even is okay or important" in a more narrow context, it may be acceptable to get even with a large corporation, but not be appropriate to get even with an individual. The two ideas are quite different; the variations in the interpretation and application of schemas is crucial. We might observe someone respond very calmly to a particular situation but see that same individual react angrily to what appears to be an identical situation. People might note the same of you. The meaning of the situation is interpreted differently at different times and in different contexts. They may see you respond one way one day and very differently the next day. And while they may see the two situations as basically the same, you may see them as being very different and, as a result, calling for a different response.

Schemas may also be active or inactive. Active schemas govern your day-to-day behavior—for example, how to respond to a compliment ("thank you") or a criticism ("drop dead"). Inactive schemas are dormant until they are stimulated by some internal or external stress. As we noted earlier, a dormant schema may be "Eat anything to survive." This would be triggered into activity by the stressor of approaching starvation. If you are just hungry, you will probably maintain your normal ideas about what foods are appropriate to eat. The belief that "I will eat anything to survive" will return to its dormant state when the stress of starvation is no longer present. By reducing your stress and the situations that create stress, you can make sure that your inactive schemas remain inactive.

Vulnerablity Factors

A number of factors will make you more vulnerable to certain stressors and, thereby, to certain schemas. We call these *vulnerability factors*. Vulnerability factors decrease your ability to put things aside and stay calm. They make you more likely to interpret situations and circumstances as stressful, and to respond to situations that you were previously able to ignore. If several vulnerability factors are operative simultaneously, it is more likely that you will become sensitive and vulnerable. The more sensitive and vulnerable you become, the lower your threshold becomes. The lower your threshold, the more likely you are to respond, possibly in an explosive manner. These vulnerability factors include things like acute health problems (e.g., the flu), chronic illness (e.g., respiratory problems), chronic pain, deterioration of health (e.g., aging), hunger, anger, fatigue, loneliness, or any major life loss (e.g, death of a spouse), any major life change (e.g., a child being born), substance abuse, poor problem-solving abilities, poor impulse control, aftereffects of any traumatic event (e.g., posttraumatic stress disorder), and psychological vulnerability (e.g., depression).

How the Vulnerability Factors Work

A single schema may be responsible for generating a broad range of thoughts, feelings, and behaviors. For example, the schema "To be loved (or approved of, accepted, or cherished), I must be perfect" might generate a number of thoughts and behaviors in both work and relationship areas. You might become a perfectionist in order to increase the probability that other people will like you, think that you are better than others, or praise you. On the other hand, the schema might be specific either to work or to interpersonal issues. Overall, however, when you are more vulnerable, you may be far more responsive to a particular situation, react more quickly to a comment, place greater weight on your thoughts, and find the schema far more compelling than you do when you have a higher threshold.

Because schemas are the basis for our understanding of the world, they are also the source of our everyday internal dialogue. When schemas generate negative and derogatory thoughts about yourself, your world, or your future, you have the essential ingredients for depression. If your schemas generate fear or concern about your personal safety or the safety of your home and children, you might experience anxiety.

This self-derogatory life view ("I'm no good") is something that you probably learned as a child. In the context of a group, it may be part of a broader cultural sense of inferiority ("We're no good"). Parents, teachers, family members, friends, and peers not only help form schemas, but help maintain them (regardless of whether the effect is negative or positive, or whether they hold any truth). Families view the world through their own cultural filters, which have to do with basic rules regarding sexual behavior, food, education, reactions to other racial, ethnic, or religious groups, and religious beliefs. If an individual within a family attempts to change the family belief system or alter the strength of a particular family belief, the family may mobilize to shut out the heretic or try to convince the individual to accept the family belief in question.

Some family-based schemas appear across cultures. For example, many of us learned to eat everything on our plates because we were told that "children are starving in. . . ." The rule "Eat everything on your plate" may persist long after we've left home. Rules about eating easily can be traced to parents and their direct instructions or modeling. The essential therapeutic question is not *where* the behavior comes from, but what keeps the schema active over many years.

"Good" Schemas versus "Bad" Schemas

Schemas in and of themselves are not necessarily good or bad. It is instead your interpretation or expression of a schema that determines whether you behave in a manner that causes you trouble, brings you satisfaction, or just doesn't meet your needs. If we look at the belief "I am unable to function well without the active support of others," we can question whether you are a dependent person. The point

is not whether being dependent in and of itself is good or bad. (For example, being dependent might motivate you to seek a supportive, helpful partner or choose a career that offers great support or it might keep you in an abusive relationship.) Rather, the pain is whether that dependence is causing you to behave in positive or negative ways. Schemas often shift from being adaptive to being maladaptive. This usually occurs when individuals have functioned well for most of their lives but experience a life change. Particular schemas may not adapt well to the change and subsequently become maladaptive in coping with the new circumstances. The following example illustrates this point.

> Alan was a 67-year-old male. He had recently retired from his position as the chief executive officer (CEO) of a large international firm. He began working in the company's mailroom when he was a high school student, and over a period of 50 years had gradually worked himself up to CEO. In his retirement he was physically healthy, well-off financially, and had good marital and family relationships and a circle of friends. When he came in for therapy, however, he was severely depressed. The schemas that drove him to succeed were "I am what I do or produce," "One is judged by one's productivity," and "If one isn't working, one is lazy and worthless." These beliefs served him well while he was working and producing. Now that he was retired, those same beliefs were contributing to his depression. In other words, the schemas were the same, but their effect on his life was far different.

Whisper-Down-the-Lane

Our reactions are based on how we sense, perceive, and interpret information. Because we all have our own ways of sensing, perceiving, and interpreting the world around us, we each funnel incoming information through our own biased system. Our reactions, therefore, are derived primarily out of a system formed by our own memories, feelings, and prior reactions. A helpful way to understand how this works is to think of the child's game of Whisper-Down-the-Lane. The game begins with one person whispering something to the next person, who then whispers their understanding of that information to the next person. By the time the secret reaches the end of the line, it has been changed. The child's initial statement (incoming information) becomes distorted by the next child (his or her own cognitive process). Because Whisper-Down-the-Lane is a game, these distortions result only in fun. In real life, our processes of interpretation ultimately result in certain behaviors and responses that have important consequences for our happiness and well-being.

SCHEMA CHANGE

Schemas are constantly in evolution. From our earliest years, previously formed schemas are altered and new schemas are developed to meet the increasingly complex demands of the world. As an infant, your perceptions were governed by your limited interaction with your world—your crib and the few people who took care of you. As you developed additional skills of mobility and began looking around, crawling, and then walking, you probably perceived your world as significantly broader, both in scope and complexity. Because of your increased interaction with the world, you began to incorporate family-related and cultural schemas. If you were ignored or hurt as a child you might have developed beliefs about the meaning of a lack of love and support from others. You might believe "Nobody is available to meet my needs."

One way of understanding how a schema changes is to see it as the interaction between two processes. The processes are

1. interpreting the world through existing schemas, and

2. interpreting the world through changing and modifying our schemas.

First, we tend to react to the world in terms of our existing schemas. If we can apply old schemas successfully, there is no need to change them. If, however, those rules fail to work, we try to make tiny adjustments. If that change works, there is no need to make further change, at least for the time being. If, however, the tiny adjustment does not work, we try to make increasingly larger changes until we are able to meet successfully the demands of the new situation. Problems arise when we persist in using old beliefs without refitting them to the new circumstances in which we are involved. We may end up using them without measuring how appropriate they are to new situations.

Schemas are often difficult to alter because they are comprised of five factors of differing proportions. The importance or saliency of each of the factors is different for each person. One or many factors might also change its relative importance, depending upon the schema involved, the situation, and the person.

1. There is a strong *emotional* component. A particular belief or belief system may engender a great deal of emotion and be emotionally bound to past experience.

2. The length of the *time* the schemas have been held affects how easily they can be changed. Schemas that are "old" or have been part of your personal history for many years will be more powerful and harder to change.

3. It is important from *whom* you acquired the schema. The more important (and credible) the source, the more powerful the schema will be for you.

4. The *cognitive* element of the schema accounts for how it pervades your thoughts and images. The schemas can be described in great detail by identifying the particular thoughts that occur in relation to them.

5. There is also a *behavioral* component, which involves the way the belief system governs your responses to a particular situation or circumstance.

In order to alter schemas that have endured for a long period of time, are strongly believed, and were learned from a significant and credible source, it is necessary to examine the belief from as many different perspectives as possible. A strictly cognitive strategy (focusing solely on one's thoughts) would have less impact on one's actual emotional responses and behaviors. Similarly, focusing only on one's emotional or behavioral components neglects the cognitive realm. Viewing any of these three areas in isolation can limit the overall impact of the therapeutic process.

You may describe yourself as displaying particular characteristics as far back as you can remember. Objective observation by your friends and family may support your views that you have behaved in a certain way from early childhood. For most of us a particular set of core schemas is well established in early- to middle-childhood (ages 5 to 8). So how can you determine which schemas are moderate in strength (and thus capable of being changed) and which schemas are powerful (and probably unchangeable)? The following list can help you make this determination. If the belief fits the following criteria, it is probably less capable of being changed.

- In addition to the core belief, you maintain many other related beliefs that are definitely unchangeable.
- The belief is still powerfully reinforced by your parents, friends, or significant others.
- Although the belief is not particularly reinforced by others, an attempt to change it will not be reinforced or may even be punished; for example, you believe that changing the belief will result in others' not liking you, accepting you, or loving you as much.
- Although the belief has not explicitly been connected to feelings of worthlessness, any attempts to act in a "worthwhile" way or to be successful would be ignored by the very people whom you would like to respond to you.
- Your parents or significant others discourage you from entertaining the changed or altered beliefs; for example, when you believe you've done something good and want to tell people about it, you are told that "It's not nice to brag" or "You shouldn't toot your own horn because people will think less of you."

HOW TO USE THIS BOOK

This workbook is designed to help you address the areas in your life that are problematic for you. Not every chapter will apply to you, but you should read each chapter's introduction and vignettes to determine if the chapter can be helpful. Each of the chapters focuses on a certain type of problem or symptom of BPD. The symptom is described in detail and examples (in the form of vignettes) are offered. Your therapist will also be reading the introductions and the vignettes, and he or she will discuss with you how you felt and reacted to the vignettes. If you find yourself relating to the vignettes or can identify the chapter topic as a personal problem, completing the worksheets in that chapter may be helpful. These worksheets are designed to assess your own patterns in relation to each of the characteristics of BDP, provide assignments, and define interventions that you can utilize. The worksheets will also help you assess the severity of the problem, understand how the symptoms are manifesting, and define the interventions that you can utilize. Before you begin reading the chapters and completing the worksheets, however, you should understand some of the basic components of treatment in general.

Self-Monitoring of Perceptions, Automatic Thoughts, & Situations

Some of the worksheets prompt you to self-monitor. You can think of self-monitoring as a means of understanding how you perceive the world. (Your therapist will help you better understand this term.) Self-monitoring is a method in which you can learn more about yourself and ultimately glean important information that can be utilized in your treatment. Self-monitoring can be described as watching and viewing yourself to see how you respond, think, feel, and physically react to certain events or situations. Sometimes we go through life on autopilot, unaware of how we have become involved in a situation. Self-monitoring helps you become more self-conscious; you learn to read your own signals as they are sent by your body, mind, emotions, and behaviors.

Self-monitoring provides a valuable window onto our behaviors and also gives your therapist something tangible to work with in creating a program that will work for you. You can utilize information that you have obtained from self-monitoring as a means of predicting how you may react or respond to a given situation. Once you understand your patterns, you can monitor yourself to determine what is problematic for you. Then you can protect yourself, alter your behaviors, or even try something different as a means of coping with the situation.

Self-monitoring means listening to your body's own internal alarm system, which, when activated, allows you to control the events that subsequently happen. How does this process begin? We begin by sensing through our basic system of five senses. Our sensory system is designed to physically detect things in the world around us. We use our senses of sight, hearing, touch, taste, and smell to pick up signals from our environment. Each of the senses sends messages to our brain, which then perceives the information and gives it meaning. By perceiving, we actually understand or define what is happening around us. We can then make decisions based on learning, experience, and patterns of thought, (or schemas) that have been developing since we were born (and maybe before). Remember, however, that as information becomes available to us, it has gone through our own filters;—filters created by both early and ongoing experiences. From our perceptions, we act. For example, your eyes may sense a large furry animal with jagged teeth running toward you. This image is sent to your brain, which perceives a dangerous animal that could cause harm. Your reaction to that perception is to run.

Generally, we take in the environment, form schema, generate perceptions, and, ultimately, create solutions that will meet our needs and assure our safety. We also, ideally, tend to follow societal standards in behavior. As children, we create patterned ways of perceiving and therefore responding to certain situations; these patterns of perceiving influence and sometimes directly determine how we react in certain situations. But individual patterns are not necessarily appropriate in every context and some patterns outlive their usefulness entirely. If, for example, a child has been hit by an adult several times, his or her perception of someone yelling may cause extreme fear and a desire to hide. As adults, we can't hide when someone is angry. So our learned pattern, although necessary to protect ourselves when growing up, may no longer be useful or relevant when we are full grown.

Self-monitoring brings these patterns—good and bad, helpful and unhelpful—into focus.

Self-monitoring is nothing complicated or esoteric. We all self-monitor every day. As children we learn to monitor what we say to our teachers, parents, and friends. We continue to watch ourselves as adults. The goal of self-monitoring, therefore, is to learn how you sense, perceive, and react to situations and experiences. Again, we're all different. Self-monitoring will assist you in predicting situations that may distress you, and in knowing how you may react. The goal of self-monitoring in the context of the Taking Control program is to understand yourself better and, with the information you have learned about yourself, to help define specific treatment interventions aimed at changing the reactions with which you aren't happy or that have given you problems. Once you begin to identify the problematic areas and responses that you wish to address, you, just by being aware that a problem exists, are beginning to take control.

If you attempt to change or challenge your held schemas or rules, you may get angry and/or you may experience great anxiety. Schemas provide basic structure to your personality. As you begin to challenge them, your system might react to protect what it is used to doing. Although the schematic structure that you use to define yourself may not always be how you wish it would be, it has provided and continues to provide structure and protection against the world and against the unknown. Sticking to your known rules and schemas minimizes anxiety. By

stepping outside the rules and challenging yourself, you become vulnerable. Sometimes taking risks can cause feelings of anxiety or fear, which might accompany your feelings of vulnerability.

When people become anxious they respond in one of three ways: Fight, flight, or freeze. Since prehistoric times, our bodies are programmed biologically to react to threats (physical or mental) in order to protect ourselves and survive.

- You might *fight* or go directly against any challenges you and your therapist initiate.
- You might want to *flee* and not wish to further challenge yourself.
- You might, in an attempt to protect yourself, wish to avoid the whole thing and forget you wanted to challenge your held patterns.
- You might feel stuck or *frozen*. You may feel helpless in the face of change and get stuck in those feelings.

These are all normal responses. With the help of your therapist you can work through them and prevent them from disrupting your efforts to live the life that you want to live. Usually these reactions are temporary and, as you begin to practice new ways and means of viewing and reacting to things, your fight, flight, and freeze reactions will likely soon dissipate.

Setting Treatment Goals

Obviously, if you only partially subscribe to a particular belief, it is going to be much easier for you to give it up. This is because you are only giving up a small piece of your belief system as opposed to challenging what you see and regard as "yourself." As you continue through the workbook, it is important that you consider what you *really* want to change. (Your therapist will be working with you to define your treatment goals.) Completing treatment goals doesn't mean that you will lose who you are as a person. On the contrary, working with your therapist to identify the areas you wish to work on will help you continue to learn, develop, and grow as a person. Together with your therapist, you can achieve the overall treatment goals, as well as the individual goals in each chapter.

Suggested Interventions

Once you have identified your goals and what you wish to work on, each chapter will suggest some interventions. These interventions will help you achieve your goals. Following are the most common interventions.

PHYSICAL

1. *Stop.* Dysfunctional thoughts often have a snowball effect. They tend to accumulate and elicit a "second string" of dysfunctional thoughts. Problems may increase exponentially. If this process continues unimpeded, dysfunctional thoughts will run rampant, generating accompanying maladaptive responses. Some of these maladaptive responses can be in the form of physiological reactions, such as those created by anxiety (e.g., shortness of breath, rapid heartbeat, sweatiness, and upset stomach). Stopping is not difficult to master. WORKSHEET 4: THE DYSFUNCTIONAL THOUGHT RECORD (DTR; Beck, 1995) will help you identify which thoughts generate maladaptive responses. You can then flag yourself when those thoughts occur and simply interrupt the flow of thoughts with a sudden stimulus (imagined or real), which will prompt you to begin thinking other thoughts. (For example, you can utilize a visual, auditory, or tactile interruptive stimulus—such as imagining a stop sign, hearing the word *stop*, or snapping a rubber band against your wrist—when the thought occurs [Beck, 1995].) This interrupts the physical sensations that arise from dysfunctional thoughts.

2. *Relax.* Relaxation and breathing exercises can bring considerable relief to an anxious and/or tense individual. Often the physical sensations that accompany anxiety can worsen the anxiety. Progressive muscle relaxation (PMR) techniques, first demonstrated by Jacobson (1962), have been proven to decrease anxiety. PMR is easily taught in your therapist's office and, once you learn it, you can utilize the technique at home. Relaxation techniques can be taught with a variety of accessory methods, including visual or auditory imagery combined with practiced breathing exercises (Freeman, Pretzer, Fleming, & Simon, 1990). Bernstein and Borkovec (1976) provide a good primer for those who are not familiar with these widely-used techniques.

3. *Relaxing Imagery.* In combination with the previous two techniques, employing relaxing imagery can decrease physiological arousal and subsequent anxiety. If you are able to identify a safe, relaxing image or scene (e.g., a beach or a wooded area), you can utilize that image in conjunction with stopping and relaxation techniques. Self-recorded audiotapes that describe your scene or play soothing music or sounds can be combined with visualizing your relaxing

image (Freeman et al., 1990). The following prompts can be used to assist you in defining your imagery.

I feel safe imagining _____

_____.

I hear _____

_____.

I feel _____

_____.

I can see _____

_____.

I can smell _____

_____.

I can taste _____

_____.

My safe person who can join me here is _____

_____.

EMOTIONAL

1. *Scale Back.* Because you are an exceptionally sensitive person, it would be unrealistic for you to try not to experience the emotions that accompany stress. You can, however, try to scale them back. Consider when you are experiencing a stressful situation turning those anxious feelings down a notch. Think of baking a soufflé. If the oven is too hot, the soufflé will overheat. If you yourself overheat, you may do or say something that you later regret. Before you react to the feelings you are experiencing, try to turn yourself down a few degrees—just like the oven. You can then learn to take control of what you consider to be damaging aspects of your relationships. Begin by rating the severity of emotion you are experiencing. Once you have tried to scale down your emotional response, take a moment to rate your emotion again and note the difference in the ratings. Scaling back takes practice. Do not be discouraged if you are unable to turn yourself down as quickly as you'd like to.

2. *Improving Communication of Feelings.* Madonna sings, "Express yourself, then you know your love is real." However, expressing yourself is not always an easy feat. If throughout your life you have not always received positive reactions to your expression of feelings, you might have learned that saying or showing what you feel is not safe. However, in adulthood, those old ways of viewing your self-expression might be hindering you from being in a completely truthful relationship. How can you learn to express your feelings? By learning to communicate better.

Communication is a three-step process.

It begins with the *sender* of the message; this is the person trying to tell or show the other person something.

Then there is the actual *message* itself.

The message itself is meant to reach the *receiver* of the information.

Remember the filter system described earlier? The sender wants to say something to the receiver. However, the original message is subject to the sender's filter system. So, although the sender may have something very kind to say to the other person, the sender's body language or tone of voice actually might be saying something else, (e.g., disinterest). The sender's eye contact might be poor, or he or she might be doing something else that gives the appearance of disinterest. The message transmitted is shaped by the sender's filter system, so it might have more than one meaning. The receiver then picks up this message. However, in the process of being picked up, the message is again interpreted through the receiver's own filtering system.

As you can see, much misunderstanding can result from a simple exchange of words. Listen to a conversation. Often you will hear "Oh, I thought you meant . . . " "But you said . . . " "I don't remember it that way . . . " or "you mean what?"

COGNITIVE

1. *Challenge Catastrophic Thinking.* This form of thinking assumes the worst is going to happen. You might believe that when a situation arises, a catastrophy is the most likely scenario. Challenge those catastrophic thoughts. Is it likely that the dreaded event will happen? Are you reacting to a catastrophy that has occurred only in your mind?

2. *Black-and-White Thinking.* This form of thinking considers things in an all-or-nothing way. Tending to extremes, there is very little "gray" in this form of thinking; this means that many opportunities might be overlooked. Think of an artist's palette. Imagine that the palette has only black and white paint. However, if the artist mixes black and white, a range of grays results. Consider looking at the grays of life instead of just the blacks and whites. The grays in life are all of the options or alternatives that you have at your disposal.

3. *Weigh the Evidence.* Do you make assumptions without looking at the proof? You might rush to conclusions that cannot be substantiated by actual evidence. Try to challenge yourself to produce evidence of the feared event. Try to prove yourself wrong or prove the unlikelihood that the worst is happening or will happen. Think of yourself as a scientist gathering data to support (or refute) your conclusion. The chapters will provide charts for you to complete where you will list the apparent proof of your conclusions and the corresponding refuting statements. You might want to carry your charts with you in case you need to be reminded of more positive outcomes.

4. *Consider the Consequences.* Challenge yourself to examine your behaviors before you act. This requires you to read your physical and emotional warning signs and ask yourself to identify the positive and negative consequences of the behavior.

5. *Avert Impulsivity.* You will be asked to fill in the IMPULSIVITY CHART (Pretzer, 1990). This requires you to:

a. *Identify the impulse.* Watch and monitor yourself—physically, emotionally, cognitively, and behaviorally—for impulses.

b. *Inhibit automatic responses.* What are the positives and negatives of acting upon a certain urge or impulse? How do they weigh out? For instance, does a night of sexual passion outweigh the possibility of danger with a stranger? When we enter situations, we usually have a preconception about how they will turn out. This is a result of our experiences growing up as well as functioning in everyday society. For instance, we know that if we park in a no-parking zone, we might be able to get into the store more quickly (positive) but we are also likely to get a ticket (negative). Often, we can predict an outcome just by examining the situation in more detail and by taking the time to read and monitor ourselves better.

c. *Identify the alternatives.* Now that you have made an informed choice about your urges, does that mean you'll never have fun again? Of course not. It's all a matter of degree, of finding the middle ground. For example, how could you avoid placing yourself in a dangerous situation but continue to make a connection with a person you have just met? What are your alternatives?

d. *Select a response.* Identify and challenge fears related to alternatives. How do you make the choice to act or not to act? What are your expectations regarding the act? What are the hopes related to carrying out your impulse? What, if any, are your fears about not acting on an urge? Does actually looking before you leap make you boring, unalive? These responses need to be

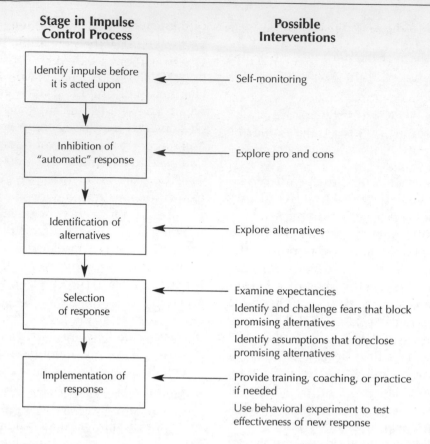

Stage in Impulse Control Process	Possible Interventions
Identify impulse before it is acted upon	Self-monitoring
Inhibition of "automatic" response	Explore pro and cons
Identification of alternatives	Explore alternatives
Selection of response	Examine expectancies Identify and challenge fears that block promising alternatives Identify assumptions that foreclose promising alternatives
Implementation of response	Provide training, coaching, or practice if needed Use behavioral experiment to test effectiveness of new response

*(Adapted from J. Pretzer [1990]. *Borderline personality disorder.* In A. Beck, A. Freeman, & Associates [eds.], *Cognitive Therapy of Personality Disorders* [pp. 176–207]. New York: Guilford Press. Reprinted by permission of the Guilford Press.)

challenged, as acting on some urges might actually threaten your life or endanger relationships.

e. *Implement a response.* This final step entails actually choosing a response. If you are learning to take control of your impulses, it will take practice, training, and learning to identify your vulnerable times when you're most likely to do something you might later regret.

How can you ensure that you follow this five-step decision-making process? By examining the physical, cognitive, and affective aspects of yourself and your situation. This will provide you with some additional support as you attempt to take control of your behaviors and your impulsivity.

6. *Common-Sense Questions.* When you ask yourself common-sense questions such as "Could this really be happening?" or "Could I be reading this wrong?" you challenge your beliefs about what you are perceiving or experiencing.

7. *Reflect on Previous Experiences.* Consider whatever situation is making you feel uncomfortable. Have you been in a similar situation in the past? What was the result of that situation?

BEHAVIOR

1. *Think of the Consequences.* What is or could be the consequence of your behavior? Many times you have found yourself experiencing difficulty due to not foreseeing the consequences of your behaviors. Try using means–end thinking. In other words, is what you are meaning to do going to give you the end you want? Consider the behavior and ask yourself, "Is it worth it? Is it for the good of myself and/or my relationship?"

2. *Try Something Different.* Identify and try a different behavior. For example, instead of yelling at your significant other when you are upset, try to maintain a normal speaking tone. Once you have listed alternative ways of acting in a situation, carry that list around with you.

3. *Remove Yourself.* Sometimes you might feel as if you are not going to be able to control what you do. Don't give yourself the opportunity to lose control. Try taking a walk, going into another room, or letting whomever you might be having problems with know that you might not be able to discuss something at that moment because you are too upset. At this juncture, you need to cool down. This

will help you avoid saying or doing something that you might later regret.

4. *Stop What You're Doing.* Take a moment to stop. We tend to experience physiological sensations as a reaction to something we perceive. Once you recognize that you are experiencing those familiar "butterflies in the stomach" take a moment to just stop. By allowing yourself a moment of not doing, analyzing, thinking, or reacting, you give your body a chance to regain its equilibrium and help yourself calm down. Take a seat, take a breath, and focus on nothing but taking control.

5. *Relax.* Behavioral relaxation techniques are identical to the physical relaxation techniques described earlier. Feelings of anger, anxiety, or upset respond well to relaxation techniques after you have stopped and taken a moment to be still. If possible, sit down in a comfortable chair. Relax all of your muscles and let the chair hold your weight. Calmly breathe in deeply, focusing on your diaphragm filling up and exhaling air. Do this three times. Imagine yourself beginning to relax and starting to take control. In this way you can stop the cycle of undesirable behavior.

6. *Relaxing Imagery.* While you are stopping and relaxing your muscles, imagine yourself in a very comfortable place or a place you love to visit. Some people like to imagine themselves on a beach or in a forest. Whatever makes you relax—think of that scene. Think of the smells, feel the breezes, and hear the sounds; imagine what all of the sensations feel like. Once you have relaxed, you have better control and are better able to examine your feelings, thoughts, and behaviors. You are gaining control and helping your body and mind relax.

7. *Identify a Friend (Safe Person).* If you are able to identify the times that are especially difficult for you, it is imperative that you identify someone who is close to you, supportive, and understands that you might at times be struggling for self-control. This person should be your *safe person*, someone you can turn to who generally doesn't cause you more distress. Try to carry the person's phone number with you. You might even want to have a code word you can say so that, even if you lack privacy, the person knows that you need to talk.

KEEPING YOUR SENSITIVITY IN MIND

All of your life, you have probably understood yourself as sensitive. You might be more sensitive to pain than other people, so that an appointment at the dentist is a far more powerful experience for you. You might cry more easily at a movie or when you hear about a sad event. You might be more sensitive to the subtle cues of human interaction that less sensitive people never even notice. For many people, being sensitive to others is a blessing, but it might have become a curse for you. You might respond to things that other people do not notice and then get told to "calm down" or to "back off." This sensitivity is something that we will be talking about throughout this program.

SUMMARY

If you have BPD, your life is full of instability. You might feel misunderstood, alone, and empty. The symptoms of BPD pervade all aspects of your life, including how you react, behave, feel, think, and experience life. These basic tendencies occur in a similar way across situations and have at some point caused distress and discomfort. If you want to address your patterns of unstable relationships, moods, and self-image, the Taking Control Program can help you uncover the schemas beneath these patterns. Once you have identified the patterns and their underlying schemas, you then have the option to change them. By understanding and directly targeting schemas, you can more effectively resolve life crises and positively affect how you feel, act, and think.

The therapeutic steps are:

1. identifying your particular problematic areas;

2. identifying your schemas;

3. exploring schemas to understand their value and power;

4. identifying the thoughts, behaviors, and ideas that maintain particular schemas;

5. identifying which schema-derived reactions you wish to change;

6. and structuring specific interventions based on your personal, family-related, and cultural schemas.

By confronting, disputing, or responding more adaptively to powerful, long-held schemas and to their emotional, behavioral, and cognitive consequences, you can begin to cope better and move in more productive directions.

CHAPTER 1

Loneliness:
Avoiding Being Alone
& Isolated

As young children, many of us experience fears of being left alone or of being separated from those whom we love or about whom we care. If we were to observe small children on the playground starting to establish independence from their parents (usually the mother), we would see children gradually tolerating more and more time away from or at a distance from their parents. We may see children run across the playground to play with others, while frequently looking back to make sure their parents are still there. Parents act as a safe "home-base" that children can return to when they become tired or stressed, and are ready to be cared for again. If these early explorations away from parents are successful, children end up feeling comfortable being out of the direct view of their parents and later, as adults, feel comfortable being alone.

We may continue to have fears about being alone as we go through adolescence and the early adult years. We generally look to others to care for us, nurture us, and make sure that our needs for companionship are met. As we grow older, we become more able to tolerate those times when others who are important to us are not as immediately available as we may want. We may never really like it, but we learn to accept it. If, however, the early explorations that we made as young children were unsuccessful, and our parents were not there for us when we

needed them as adults we might be extremely sensitive to being alone.

As we grow and develop, we all experience painful times when we are left alone, uncared for, or rejected. Sometimes we end up feeling alone even in the middle of a crowd or in the middle of a family gathering. As adults we may have become keenly sensitive to any loss, or even to the slightest hint of separation from others who are important to us. As a sensitive person, you have throughout life developed ways of learning and predicting when you may be left or learned to read signs that "something bad may come." People with BPD may search relentlessly for signs of reassurance or make repeated attempts to form connections or to restore connections they fear are broken or in the process of breaking. This sensitivity to loss may motivate you to think and feel in ways you normally wouldn't regarding other life experiences. You might behave in ways that seem to others as if you are attempting to force people (whether they are loved ones or more casual acquaintances) not to leave. Your loved ones might or might not actually be leaving, but the mere thought of being deserted becomes the driving force of your thoughts, feelings, and actions. The result is that in your frantic efforts to avoid being alone or deserted, you might actually get exactly the opposite of what you hoped—You might push away those for whom you care, or you might lash out against those whom you perceive are leaving or who have already left. The result is that your worst fear is often realized.

VIGNETTES

Does anything in either of the following examples sound familiar to you?

Vignette 1: Amy

All Amy could think was, "I can't believe this is happening again!" Feeling upset and desperate, she sat by the phone and shakily dialed John's number. It was the third call that day. Her heart pounded in her chest. She was breathing so hard she wasn't sure she'd be able to talk, let alone make sense. He was going away without her on a two-day fishing trip with his friends. John finally answered the phone after four rings, but it seemed like an eternity.

"John, it's me. Honey, listen, I love you and I need you to cancel your trip. I absolutely have to see you this weekend."

John replied, "Amy, we've been through this again and again. I've been planning this trip for weeks. The arrangements have been made, I've paid for it, and the guys are counting on me; it's too late to back out now."

Suddenly her fear shifted to rage. "Goddammit John, we've been spending every weekend together for the past three months!" All she could see was red. She stopped planning what to say and the words just tumbled out. Demand followed insult. As her rage intensified, so did her use of profanity. John hung up after Amy threatened to end the relationship if he didn't stay with her that weekend. The last thing he said was that he welcomed the breakup.

"You bastard!" Amy said to the dead phone. Sobbing, she threw the phone across the room.

Vignette 2: Emily

The uneasiness Emily felt in her stomach was quickly changing to sensations of dread as she thought about what Mike wanted to say to her. His message on her answering machine said something about a change in their usual meeting time on Saturday night. She noticed her hands quivering as she poured a glass of water to relieve the dryness in her mouth. The lump in her throat made it hard to swallow. "What if he doesn't want to see me anymore? He's the only one who has ever really understood me. I'm not sure if I can go on without him!" she thought. Almost breathless, she repeatedly pushed her redial button every 30 seconds after her initial call to him and paged her therapist at least ten times.

Review the Vignettes

Does anything in the vignettes sound familiar? Do the circumstances seem to fit your style of behavior or your experience? Perhaps you have felt these things but haven't reacted as dramatically as the characters did. Keep in mind the important features of these examples. Both Amy and Emily had intense fears that their loved ones were leaving them or changing the status of their relationship. Most importantly, Amy and Emily sensed (heard) information from their significant others and perceived that something very negative or very bad was going to happen. Their automatic thoughts were based on the schema that "If something changes, they must be leaving me." These automatic thoughts led them to jump to frightening conclusions. Both Amy and Emily began to think, feel, and behave in manners that might not have been what they actually intended. Ultimately their behaviors worked contrary to their desires. Amy had angry outbursts of rage and profanity, and Emily made frantic efforts to contact Mike. In other words, they ended up pushing their partners away

Note the warning signs that came from the characters' alarm systems. These warning signs were in the form of physical, emotional, cognitive, and behavioral responses. Both characters experienced their fear and anger in uncomfortable bodily sensations such as a lump in the throat, heart-pounding anxiety, difficulty breathing, tightness in the chest or stomach, and/or incredible tension. They tended to assume the worst would happen, and viewed the situation in an all-or-nothing fashion. Additionally, their fears led to behaviors they later regretted.

WHAT YOU WOULD LIKE TO CHANGE

First, discuss with your therapist whether this seems to be an area that is problematic for you. Do you relate to the vignettes? Does this behavior appear to occur in a pattern? Is it an area of your life over which you wish you had more control? If it does not seem pertinent, discuss with your therapist whether you need to continue to the assessment section.

SELF MONITORING: HOW DO I KNOW WHAT MY PERCEPTIONS ARE?

The way to self-monitor and understand how you perceive things is to look at the feelings, thoughts, behaviors, and sensations that occur when you are experiencing the fear of being left behind or left alone. If you learned early in life that those who mean the most to you tend to leave or reject you, your emotional antenna will be up. You might frequently (if not constantly) scan the horizon and be especially sensitive to any hints or clues that indicate that others might be leaving you. This creates a pattern in which you perceive situations as dangerous when in actuality they might not be.

The key word here is *again*. For example, Amy, in the first vignette, might have learned as a young child that if a significant person leaves for extended periods of time, that person might not return. When Mike wanted to go on a fishing trip, Amy perceived this event as dangerous; that is, she believed she was being left *again* and that he might never return. That would mean that Amy would be left alone *again*.

THE WORKSHEETS

The following section includes several worksheets that address the current chapter topic. The worksheets are designed to help you learn more about yourself so that you can decide if there is anything you wish to change. Your therapist can help you use them.

WORKSHEET 1
The Assessment

Rate the severity of the following problems as you think they may relate to you.

0 = none   1 = mild   2 = moderate   3 = severe   4 = extremely severe

1. There are times when I feel that I cannot tolerate being alone. ____

2. I often worry that the people close to me will leave me. ____

3. I find it distressing when others make changes in our plans. ____

4. I become obsessed with the threat that someone close to me may leave. ____

5. If other people reject me, I believe that I am bad, unlovable, or worthless. ____

6. I believe that if I'm not involved in a relationship, nothing matters. ____

7. I feel compelled to make repeated attempts to contact someone even when I've left messages. ____

8. I worry that I can't survive unless I have someone to depend on. ____

9. I continuously seek reassurance to allay my fears of rejection. ____

10. I force others to stay with me by acting out or saying inappropriate things. ____

If you rated several of these items as representing the way you often think or feel, you might be especially sensitive to being rejected or deserted by the ones you love or about whom you care. This sensitivity might lead you to feel uncomfortable relating to those with whom you interact and might also lead you to think, say, and do things you would otherwise not want to do (and that a part of you knows are not good).

WORKSHEET 2
The Assignment

Think of the last argument or "big scene" that occurred with a significant other, boyfriend, girlfriend, family member, friend, or coworker that was related to your feeling or thinking that person was going to leave you. Try to get into the moment and imagine yourself there. Use the lines below to detail your experience. Be as specific as possible. You will compile your reactions in WORKSHEET 3: THE INCIDENT CHART.

_____

_____

_____

_____

_____

_____

_____

_____

_____

_____

_____

_____

_____

_____

_____

_____

_____

_____

_____

_____

_____

_____

WORKSHEET 3
The Incident Chart*

This worksheet will help you begin uncovering the schema related to this criterion. Think about the situation you described in WORKSHEET 2 and ask yourself the following:

- What was I physically experiencing before, during, and after the situation?
- What was I feeling?
- What thoughts were running through my mind before, during, and after the situation?
- How was I behaving? [*name some specific behaviors*]

Now fill out the worksheet in as much detail as possible.

Situation: _____

_____

Prior to Incident

Physiological sensations	Emotions	Cognitions/ thoughts	Behaviors

During Incident

Physiological sensations	Emotions	Cognitions/ thoughts	Behaviors

After Incident

Physiological sensations	Emotions	Cognitions/ thoughts	Behaviors

*(Adapted from J. S. Beck, *Cognitive Therapy: Basics and Beyond.* Guilford Press, 1995©.)

WORKSHEET 4
The Dysfunctional Thought Record (DTR)*

This worksheet is designed to assist you in identifying your automatic thoughts. Noting your automatic thoughts can help you determine what underlying schemas or beliefs relate to particular events or situations. What are your automatic thoughts relating to being left or abandoned? For example, if you believe that someone close to you is leaving you, do experience thoughts such as "I'm being left again" or "No one cares about me?" Your therapist will help you fill out the rest.

Date/Time	Situation	Automatic thought	Emotion	Adaptive response	Outcome

*(Adapted from J. S. Beck, *Cognitive Therapy: Basics and Beyond.* Guilford Press, 1995©.)

WORKSHEET 5
Schemas

What are your rules or schemas related to being abandoned or left? Take a moment to write them down.

_____

_____

_____

_____

_____

_____

_____

Choose any of these specific rules and fill in each of the columns. Indicate what the rule is, where (or whom) it comes from, what meaning it has for you, and how likely or easy it would be for you to change that rule. Once you have identified your particular schemas, how strong they are, and whether or not they can be changed, you can begin to create treatment goals.

Schema	Where it comes from	Meaning to me	Easy to change?

WORKSHEET 6
Treatment Goals

This worksheet asks you to identify your treatment goals, the symptoms that prevent you from obtaining your goals, the schemas that are associated with those goals, and the change for which you are hoping. Are you able to imagine yourself completing the goals? Complete this chart with the help of your therapist and prioritize the importance of each of these goals.

	Symptoms that prevent you from obtaining goal	Schema associated with goal	Hoped-for change	Realistic or unrealistic?	How outcome looks if goal is reached
Goal 1: **Highest priority**					
Goal 2: **High priority**					
Goal 3: **Moderate priority**					
Goal 4: **Low priority**					

The Diagnostic Profiling System (DPS)

Your therapist will help you complete this worksheet.

FREEMAN DIAGNOSTIC PROFILING SYSTEM
(© FREEMAN, 2003) REVISED EDITION

Date of Assessment: _____

Session#: _____ Evaluator: _____

Patient Name: _____ Patient#: _____ Location: _____

Birthdate: _____ Age: _____ Race: _____ Gender: _____ Birthorder: _____ Marital/Children: _____

Employment: _____ Education: _____ Disability: _____ Medication: _____

Physician: _____ Referral Question: _____

Instructions: Record the diagnosis including the code number. Briefly identify the criteria for the selected diagnosis. Working with the patient either directly as as part of the data gathering of the clinical interview, SCALE the SEVERITY of EACH CRITERION for the patient at the PRESENT TIME. Indicate the level of severity on the grid.

DIAGNOSIS (DSM/ICD) with Code:

Axis I: _____

Axis II: _____

Axis III: _____

SEVERITY OF SYMPTOMS — HIGH / MEDIUM / LOW (vertical axis, 1–10)

DESCRIPTIVE CRITERIA (horizontal axis, 0–12)

CRITERIA:

1 _____   7 _____

2 _____   8 _____

3 _____   9 _____

4 _____   10 _____

5 _____   11 _____

6 _____   12 _____

Do you believe that the above noted criteria are a reaonably accurate sample of the patient's behavior? **YES** or **NO**

If **NO**, please indicate why: _____

Are there any reasons to believe that this individual is an imminent danger to himself/herself or others? **YES** or **NO**

If **YES**, please indicate the danger: _____

(From Freeman, 1998.)

WORKSHEET 7
Physical Triggers

Physical sensations are clues to help you avoid future situations in which you perceive that you are being left or abandoned. They might be very strong messages from your body (e.g., a pounding heart, stomach problems, or a general tenseness in your muscles). Think of the experience you described in WORKSHEET 2: THE ASSIGNMENT. What were you physically experiencing before, during, and after you perceived you were being left or abandoned? You might have felt some of the following:

- queasy stomach.
- sweating/clammy skin.
- racing heart.
- tension.
- GI distress.

Use the lines below to describe your physical sensations.

_____

_____

_____

_____

_____

_____

_____

_____

_____

_____

_____

_____

_____

_____

_____

_____

WORKSHEET 8
Physical Triggers & Suggested Interventions

Three techniques can help you combat the physiological distress that occurs prior to, during, and/or after experiencing what you perceive as someone abandoning you: (1) take a moment to stop; (2) employ relaxation techniques; and (3) use relaxing imagery.

Stop

In WORKSHEET 4 you identified the thoughts directly related to your experience of feeling abandoned. For this exercise, identify the thoughts that seem to be creating or exacerbating uncomfortable physical reactions. Use the lines below to write down those thoughts.

_____

_____

_____

_____

_____.

As soon as you experience a thought that is related to your physical upset, stop what you are doing. Unpleasant thoughts often can get out of control. Like a runaway freight train, the thoughts gain momentum and speed and need to be stopped! You can do this by

_____

_____

_____

_____

_____.

Relax

In WORKSHEET 3 you identified what specific physical symptoms occur when you are fearful that you are being left or abandoned. If you know what physical symptoms are related to feeling abandoned, you can utilize relaxation techniques when you experience those symptoms. You can do this by

_____

_____

_____

_____

_____.

Use Relaxing Imagery

After you have managed to stop your disturbing thoughts about being abandoned, use relaxation techniques in combination with going to a "safe place" in your mind. Your safe place might include being in the company of people with whom you feel safe and comfortable, and who would give you support if they were physically with you.

I feel safe imagining _____

_____

_____.

I hear _____

_____

_____.

I feel _____

_____

_____.

I can see _____

_____

_____.

I can smell _____

_____

_____.

I can taste _____

_____

_____.

My safe person who can join me here is _____

_____

_____.

WORKSHEET 9
Emotional Triggers

How would you describe the emotions you felt when you believed someone close to you was about to leave you? They might be very intense emotions such as sadness or anger. Often when we feel our needs aren't being met, we have a strong "gut" emotional response. We are social creatures and connections are vital to our survival. Use the emotions sections of WORKSHEETS 3 and 4 to identify some of the feelings you had when you believed you were being abandoned. They might include some of the following:

- fear.
- anger.
- sadness.
- disgust.

What were you feeling emotionally? Write down what those feelings were like.

_____

_____

_____

_____

_____

_____

_____

_____

_____

_____

_____

_____

_____

_____

_____

_____

_____

_____.

WORKSHEET 10
Emotional Triggers & Suggested Interventions

Scale Back

Pick one of the uncomfortable emotional responses you wish to address from WORKSHEET 9. On a scale of 1 to 10 (1 being least severe and 10 being most severe), rate the severity of the emotion you experienced when you perceived you were being abandoned.

1   2   3   4   5   6   7   8   9   10

As you continue to have uncomfortable emotions related to being abandoned try to scale back or "turn the oven down." You might want to combine scaling back with some relaxation techniques described in WORKSHEET 8 on physical triggers. Once you have turned yourself down, rate your emotions again.

1   2   3   4   5   6   7   8   9   10

How did you do? Were you able to turn yourself down? You'll notice that with practice, turning down your own emotional temperature becomes easier and easier. Can you describe how you are feeling now?

_____

_____

_____

_____

_____

_____

_____

_____

_____

_____

_____

_____

_____

_____

_____

_____

WORKSHEET 11
Cognitive/Automatic Thoughts

What thoughts were running through your mind before, during, and after you perceived you were being left or abandoned? What primary thought seemed to make you increasingly distressed? For example, did you think you would remain alone forever? Refer to WORKSHEET 4: THE DTR to identify the specific thoughts related to this topic. Write your responses below.

_____

_____

_____

_____

_____

_____

_____

_____

_____

_____

_____

_____

_____

_____

_____

_____

_____

_____

_____

_____

WORKSHEET 12
Cognitive/Automatic Thoughts & Suggested Interventions

As you review WORKSHEETS 4 and 11, you might notice some patterns related to your thoughts about others leaving you or changing the rules of a relationship. You might notice that you tend to catastrophize, or think in terms of radical black-or-white contrasts. You might not be weighing the evidence supporting your beliefs. Try combating these tendencies with the following interventions.

Challenge Catastrophic Thinking

Are you assuming the absolute worst? Are you catastrophizing a situation in which someone changed plans or said that he or she couldn't make it to a certain event? Fill in the chart below, noting any catastrophic thought that is related to a situation in which you experience feelings of being abandoned. Then challenge yourself to identify the noncatastrophic thought related to the event. For example, if you experience someone close to you changing plans at the last minute, do you have a catastrophic thought such as "They don't want to be friends with me anymore?" Can you then challenge that thought with an alternative but less catastrophic possibility such as "Perhaps they had difficulty making the time we set"?

The Catastrophic Thinking Chart		
Situation	**Catastrophic thought**	**Noncatastrophic thought**
_____ .	_____ .	_____ .
_____	_____	_____
_____	_____	_____
_____	_____	_____
_____	_____	_____
_____ .	_____ .	_____ .
_____ .	_____ .	_____ .

Challenge Black-and-White Thinking

Are you thinking only in terms of black and white? Do you have a hard time seeing the grays? For example, have you thought something like the following?

Your partner goes out ➔ *(means* only *that)* ➔ *you are being abandoned.*

Use your paint palette to mix the blacks and whites. What grays, or other options, are you able to come up with? For example, if your partner is late or changes plans, what explanations other than abandonment could exist? Challenge yourself to identify the grays. (Examples are provided to assist you.)

The Dichotomous Thinking Chart

Black   **Gray(s)**   **White**

|---|---|

He's leaving me.   He's late because   He's perfect.
                                    he's stuck in traffic.

_____ .   _____ .   _____ .

_____ .   _____ .   _____ .

_____ .   _____ .   _____ .

_____ .   _____ .   _____ .

I have a hard time mixing grays related to _____

_____

_____

_____

_____ .

Weigh the Evidence

Do you have proof that your partner or friend is leaving you? Think of the upsetting thought that you had when you were convinced you were being abandoned. Fill in the DISPUTATION CHART below with items of proof that the person was leaving you. Remember to challenge yourself with refuting statements. (Examples are provided to assist you.)

The Disputation Chart

Situation: *Boyfriend didn't call when he said he would.*

Belief: *Boyfriend wants to break up.*

Proof Supporting Belief
1. *Boyfriend didn't call.*
2. *Boyfriend forgot about me.*

3. _____ .

4. _____ .

5. _____ .

6. _____ .

Refuting Statement
1. *One late phone call doesn't mean the end of the relationship.*
2. *Boyfriend had busy day at work.*

3. _____ .

4. _____ .

5. _____ .

6. _____ .

WORKSHEET 13
Behavioral Triggers

What specific behaviors did you engage in before, during, and after you perceived you were being abandoned? Were you yelling at your significant other? Holding on to him or her? Shaking your fist at him or her? Making repeated phone calls? Take a moment to jot down what you were doing during this very stressful time.

Before:

Behavior 1 _____.

Behavior 2 _____.

Behavior 3 _____.

During:

Behavior 1 _____.

Behavior 2 _____.

Behavior 3 _____.

After:

Behavior 1 _____.

Behavior 2 _____.

Behavior 3 _____.

Detail as much information regarding your behaviors as possible. Use the lines below.

_____

_____

_____

_____

_____

_____

_____

_____

_____

_____.

WORKSHEET 14
Behavioral Triggers & Suggested Interventions

Scan the list you just made and identify which specific behaviors you wish to address.

Behavior 1 _____.

Behavior 2 _____.

Behavior 3 _____.

The following interventions can help you alter your behaviors in response to feeling abandoned.

Consider the Consequences

Plug the behaviors you listed into the chart below. Is the action you are considering likely to give you the result you want? Consider the behavior and ask yourself "Is it worth it?" "Is it for the good of myself and/or my relationship?"

The Negative and Positive Consequences Chart		
Behavior	Negative consequences	Positive consequences
_____.	_____.	_____.
_____.	_____.	_____.
_____.	_____.	_____.

After completing the chart, ask yourself the following:

- Do the negative consequences outweigh the positive consequences?
- Is it worth it to decrease this behavior?
- Do I want to continue this behavior?

Stop

Take a moment to stop. We all tend to experience physiological sensations in reaction to what we perceive. Once you recognize that you are experiencing that familiar sensation, take a moment to just stop. If you are having a thought like "Oh not again; someone is taking off on me," try to stop the thought. It might help to imagine a stop sign or to snap a rubber band against your wrist.

Relax

If you have become very upset or have noticed that you are responding to emotions related to feeling alone or left behind, you may be experiencing agitation or anxiousness. This usually involves some physical reaction (e.g., stomach problems, a rapid heartbeat, and/or sweating). These types of feelings and bodily reactions respond well to relaxation techniques. Try breathing deeply and relaxing in a comfortable chair.

Use Relaxing Imagery

While you stop and relax your muscles, imagine your safe place. Where do you feel safe? Be sure to think of all of the aspects of your safe place. Because you may be feeling especially alone when you believe that someone is leaving you, you may want to imagine that a "safe person" such as a good friend or confidant is with you.

I feel safe imagining _____

_____

_____.

I hear _____

_____

_____.

I feel _____

_____

_____.

I can see _____

_____

_____.

I can smell _____

_____

_____.

I can taste _____

_____

_____.

My safe person who can join me here is _____

_____

_____.

WORKSHEET 16
Situational Triggers

There are times, individuals, events, and places that cause a great deal of distress. Knowing which situations cause you difficulty can help you be prepared if a similar situation occurs; in particular, you can be on alert for your alarms. You identified your four areas of warning signs in WORKSHEET 3: THE INCIDENT CHART. Now list the situations in which you have experienced difficulty related to believing that you were being abandoned. Review WORKSHEET 1 if you need help identifying these situations.

1. _____

_____

_____ .

2. _____

_____

_____ .

3. _____

_____

_____ .

4. _____

_____

_____ .

5. _____

_____

_____ .

6. _____

_____

_____ .

WORKSHEET 17
Situational Triggers & Suggested Interventions

WORKSHEET 16 identifies the situations in which you have experienced difficulty related to believing that you were being abandoned. Although not all situations are avoidable—for example, you may have to go to the office even if it causes distress—there are some situations that you can avoid. For those that are not avoidable, you can choose to change your reactions. The following are brief descriptions of interventions that can be applied to any distressful situation.

Remove Yourself

Sometimes you may feel as if you are not going to be able to control what you do. Don't give yourself the opportunity to lose control. Try taking a walk, going into another room, or letting your partner know that you can't discuss something at that moment because you are too upset. For instance, if you know that when your partner is late returning home you become overwhelmed with anxiety, be sure that you can go somewhere where you are supported.

When things get particularly difficult, I can _____

_____

_____

_____

_____

_____

_____ .

Try Something Different

Try to identify a different way of behaving from what you're used to. For example, if you know that you feel especially anxious in between the times you see your girl- or boyfriend, instead of calling repeatedly for reassurance, do something constructive with your time. This could be a household project you've been wanting to complete or catching up with friends.

Instead of _____ [*behavior*],

I can try _____

_____

_____

_____

_____

_____ .

The DPS

Your therapist will help you complete this worksheet.

Date of Assessment: _____

FREEMAN DIAGNOSTIC PROFILING SYSTEM

(© FREEMAN, 2003) REVISED EDITION

Session#: _____ Evaluator: _____

Patient Name: _____ Patient#: _____ Location: _____

Birthdate: _____ Age: _____ Race: _____ Gender: _____ Birthorder: _____ Marital/Children: _____

Employment: _____ Education: _____ Disability: _____ Medication: _____

Physician: _____ Referral Question: _____

Instructions: Record the diagnosis including the code number. Briefly identify the criteria for the selected diagnosis. Working with the patient either directly as as part of the data gathering of the clinical interview, SCALE the SEVERITY of EACH CRITERION for the patient at the PRESENT TIME. Indicate the level of severity on the grid.

DIAGNOSIS (DSM/ICD) with Code:

Axis I: _____

Axis II: _____

Axis III: _____

SEVERITY OF SYMPTOMS — HIGH / MEDIUM / LOW (scale 1–10) vs. DESCRIPTIVE CRITERIA (0–12)

DESCRIPTIVE CRITERIA

CRITERIA:

1 _____   7 _____

2 _____   8 _____

3 _____   9 _____

4 _____   10 _____

5 _____   11 _____

6 _____   12 _____

Do you believe that the above noted criteria are a reaonably accurate sample of the patient's behavior? **YES** or **NO**

If **NO**, please indicate why: _____

Are there any reasons to believe that this individual is an imminent danger to himself/herself or others? **YES** or **NO**

If **YES**, please indicate the danger: _____

(From Freeman, 1998.)

CHALLENGING WHAT YOU KNOW & DO: TAKING CONTROL

Feeling alone or abandoned is a very frightening and powerful experience. It can be overwhelming. Relationships are intrinsic to our survival. We all want to belong or feel as if we are part of something. If that security is actually threatened or if we perceive that it is threatened, we can feel that our survival is being jeopardized. Fortunately, this is not usually true.

You can take charge of these terrorizing feelings. By understanding that your reactions might be based on your prior experiences with others leaving you or not following through on commitments, you can alter the way you to look at current situations and determine whether the same patterns are recurring. Typically what happens is the old self-fulfilling prophecy: We expect others to leave us and therefore act in ways that actually push them away. Maybe you have noticed some of these patterns in your own life. By staying on guard and attending to your alarm system, you can make an informed choice about how you want to handle things. You do not have to allow your prior experiences to dictate your present feelings, thoughts, and behaviors.

CHAPTER 2 | Relationships: Always A Challenge

Relationships are a critical part of all of our lives. We interact with others on a daily basis, first within our families, then with other children in school, and then with friends at home, school, and outside activities (scouting, church groups, clubs, or just "hanging out" at the mall or a friend's house). As adults we relate to coworkers, friends, and significant others. For some of us, forming and maintaining significant relationships can be a daunting task. For others, it might seem an impossible dream.

Perhaps in the process of growing up you had negative experiences relating to others. As a child you may have learned not to trust others. You may believe that although others care for you, or even love you, they ultimately may not be looking out for your best interests. Why do you and so many other people experience such difficulties? Perhaps as children you experienced important family members as being nurturing and loving but also somehow frightening. This person (or people) may have been warm, loving, accepting, and caring one minute and mean, inattentive, rejecting, and even harmful the next.

Some children learn the powerful and bitter lesson that adults, even family members, cannot be trusted. These adults might have been intrusive, excessively demanding, or abusive. They might have neglected these children or physically, emo-

tionally, or sexually abused them. Other adults may be untrustworthy because they knew about or suspected the abuse but offered no help or support.

These confusing relationships lead some of us to the expectation that *all* people with whom we become involved have the capacity to be simultaneously loving and frightening. Or that they can be loving and abusive at alternating times. The end result is a very complicated view of relationships, which might make our adult relationships problematic. We generally want and are expected to interact with and relate to others. However, because of our negative expectations about relationships, we might be gripped by fear, anxiety, and distrust. This means that there are few times when and very few people with whom we truly feel safe. This chapter largely addresses intimate or romantic relationships. However, the same type of intensity, difficulties, and problems that occur within romantic relationships might also be present in relations with friends and family.

Let's look at your relationships. Do you tend to view other people in the dichotomous terms of purely positive or negative? If you do, the natural tendency would be to seek out the best or the most positive aspects in others as soon as possible. Viewing the positive aspects or looking for the good in someone in the early stages of a relationship is a

41

normal part of courting and is sometimes known as passionate love. However, if you have trouble with positive/negative thinking attempt to create an immediate bond with the positive aspect of another person you might seek this bond so fervently that people may have described you as "intense." You may be intensely drawn to those you view as all-positive. This is part and parcel of your basic relationship pattern. This intensity at times may have frightened others, frightened you, and/or caused others to back away or saying, "Can we slow down?" or "You're crowding me." You might have noticed that your relationships begin with your desire to share a great deal, if not all, of your time with the other person. Or, you might feel very close to the individual after the first or second meeting and be inclined to share with him or her your secrets and deepest feelings. Strangely, this intense desire to connect may add fuel to the fire of your fear of being alone. Because this new relationship (as with so many previous relationships) seems as if it is the "best ever," you might begin to believe that it would be devastating for the relationship to end.

When do problems with your relationships begin to occur? As you are incredibly aware of and sensitive to changes in the behaviors of others, you might perceive them subtly shifting away from you (which may or may not have anything to do with you or what you are saying or doing). You might also be ignoring the possible negative aspects of the person with whom you are involved. This negative side may not be something that is necessarily bad or abusive, but may not be what you want or expect.

This is where your sensitivity may get you in trouble. If you monitor that the other person acts as if pulling away or requests for "space" as a rebuff, you might rapidly shift to being angry about what you perceive as a rejection. You might even see the other person's pulling away as an attempt to do harm to you. Perhaps when others pushed away from you before, you reacted by engaging in or even creating intense conflicts. These conflicts might have resulted (sometimes intentionally, sometimes not) in angry or rageful outbursts. You might even do something that is exactly opposite of what you ultimately desire. (For example, you might impulsively end the relationship or use physical aggression.) Your finely tuned sensitivity might make you seem to express simultaneously hate and love. These dramatic shifts and paradoxical emotions probably confuse your loved ones and must surely confuse you. As you are sensitive to and perceptive of changes or shifts in other people, you might feel easily betrayed, hurt, or rejected. This is a frequent pattern, and involves an ongoing vacillation between viewing relationships as all-good or all-bad, or good and bad at the same time.

You might find that you rarely are able to continue in a romantic relationship for more than a few months, and, if you do, it is usually a highly charged relationship with high levels of conflict. You might also have so much difficulty being separated from your significant other that it seems as if no amount of reassurance will make you feel better. Another indicator that this area could be problematic for you is a pattern of frequent changes in your set of friends.

In short, relationships are a difficult and challenging task. In fact, you might have decided to swear off relationships for good.

Does this sound familiar to you? Have you often found it difficult to be in a relationship?

VIGNETTES

Vignette 1: Sandi

Sandi was devastated. How on earth did she misjudge someone so badly? She had thought about how wonderful Pete was; so sweet, genuine, and unselfish; all day long. She knew she had found the man she would spend her life with. Driving home almost euphoric, Sandi expected that he, too, would feel her excitement about their budding relationship. As she opened her door, Pete met her in the hallway, apologizing that he had forgotten to tell her that he had dinner plans with his parents that evening. That same old feeling Sandi knew so well started to take over again. He wanted to go to his mother's for dinner and he was rejecting her. He forgot about her. He was selfish, rejecting, and mean. How could he do this to her? She had had a wonderful evening planned. Now he had ruined it! Her thoughts began to spiral into a rage. He thought more of his parents than of her. As that thought crossed her mind again and again, she picked up her coat, walked toward the door and said, "Go ahead to your parents, you mama's boy, but forget about coming home because I won't be here!" as she stormed out.

Vignette 2: Barbara

Barbara was furious. Once again Tom had asked her to entertain his business partner and his wife for dinner. Tom had just casually sauntered over and said, "Darling, do you really mind?" Barbara couldn't say no but she surely wanted to. She never could say no. Not to Tom, not to her boss, her friends, family, and especially her parents. She felt a tight feeling in her chest and had a hard time swallowing. The thought that kept spinning in her mind was that no one recognized, acknowledged, or loved her. She was just there to be used. If she didn't do what everyone wanted, she'd be alone with no one to love her, right? Barbara tried to swallow her fury, but she felt so utterly discarded and rejected that she stood in the kitchen weeping hysterically.

Review the Vignettes

Do either of these vignettes ring true for you? Both Sandi and Barbara had thoughts and feelings about how to relate to their significant others. The result?—anger, frustration, arguments, and misunderstandings. Sandi and Barbara learned that these kinds of feelings are just part of life and expressing them may not be a safe thing to do. Note the warning signs the characters experience. These warning signs were physical, emotional, cognitive, and behavioral responses—all part of Sandi's and Barbara's alarm systems. Both characters had experienced these types of situations before. How could they have better addressed their respective situations? By beginning to take control.

This chapter will help you discover new and different ways to communicate with others. You can also learn how to break the pattern of thinking of others as either all-good or all-bad. Your relationships don't have to be a revolving door spun by conflict and confusion. You can learn to help yourself, and even your partner, by discovering new ways to be together.

WHAT YOU WOULD LIKE TO CHANGE

First, discuss with your therapist whether this seems to be an area that is problematic for you. Do you relate to the vignettes? Does this behavior appear to occur in a pattern? Is it an area of your life over which you wish you had more control? If it does not seem pertinent, discuss with your therapist whether you need to continue to the assessment section.

SELF-MONITORING: HOW DO I KNOW WHAT MY PERCEPTIONS ARE?

Learning how to monitor yourself and others for clues that indicate potential problems is the first step to taking control. Once you have identified when you "don't feel right" (i.e., an alarm is triggered) or strongly disagree with others, try some new ways of communicating that discomfort or disagreement—without the usual heartache you've experienced before.

As discussed throughout this book, understanding your perceptions is an usually powerful avenue for gathering information. Remember the children's game Whisper Down the Lane? It's important for you to keep in mind that although your brain is telling you something, it may be giving you biased information; the incoming data has already been altered by your schemas. What are your typical perceptions related to relationships?

THE WORKSHEETS

The following section includes several worksheets that address the current chapter topic. The worksheets are designed to help you learn more about yourself so that you can decide if there is anything you wish to change. Your therapist can help you use them.

WORKSHEET 1
Assessment

Rate the severity of the following problems as you think they may relate to you.

0 = none   1 = mild   2 = moderate   3 = severe   4 = extremely severe

1. Your relationships largely consist of major ups and downs.   ____

2. You have found it difficult to remain in a romantic relationship for any
   length of time.   ____

3. Your sets of friends tend to change more quickly than those of most people.   ____

4. You frequently argue with your significant other.   ____

5. You resolve conflicts with others by arguing, leaving, or crying.   ____

6. You tend to believe your relationship is either wonderful or horrible.   ____

7. You use derogatory or insulting words during arguments.   ____

8. You feel completely out of control when you disagree with others.   ____

9. You tend to have exceptionally high standards for your significant other.   ____

10. You have become involved with someone extremely quickly, only to
    discover shortly thereafter that he or she wasn't right for you.   ____

How did you do? Keep in mind that relating to other people is not always easy. You might have had a time in your life when relationships seemed simple. Some parts of relationships are easier than others. If you rated several of these items as representing the way you think or feel, it could be that relationships are problematic for you. However, there are ways that you can improve how you relate to others and successfully remain in a relationship. With your therapist, determine whether you need to continue with this chapter.

WORKSHEET 2
The Assignment

Think of the last "big scene" that occurred with a significant other, boyfriend, girlfriend, family member, friend, or coworker. It should be someone with whom you have had an ongoing relationship (not a stranger). Take a few moments to identify the scene and the "triggers" to which you reacted very strongly. They might be times when you don't feel supported, when you feel left out, or when you disagree with others. Try to get into the moment and imagine yourself there. Use the lines below to detail your experience. Be as specific as possible. You will compile your reactions in WORKSHEET 3: THE INCIDENT CHART.

_____

_____

_____

_____

_____

_____

_____

_____

_____

_____

_____

_____

_____

_____

_____

_____

_____

_____

_____

_____

WORKSHEET 3
The Incident Chart*

This worksheet will help you begin uncovering the schemas related to this characteristic. Think about the situation you described in WORKSHEET 2 and ask yourself the following:

- What was I physically experiencing before, during, and after the situation?
- What was I feeling?
- What thoughts were running through my mind before, during, and after the situation?
- How was I behaving? [*name some specific behaviors.*]

Now fill out the worksheet in as much detail as possible.

Situation: _____

_____

Prior to Incident

Physiological sensations	Emotions	Cognitions/ thoughts	Behaviors
_____	_____	_____	_____
_____	_____	_____	_____
_____	_____	_____	_____
_____	_____	_____	_____

During Incident

Physiological sensations	Emotions	Cognitions/ thoughts	Behaviors
_____	_____	_____	_____
_____	_____	_____	_____
_____	_____	_____	_____

After Incident

Physiological sensations	Emotions	Cognitions/ thoughts	Behaviors
_____	_____	_____	_____
_____	_____	_____	_____
_____	_____	_____	_____

*(Adapted from J. S. Beck, *Cognitive Therapy: Basics and Beyond*. Guilford Press, 1995©.)

WORKSHEET 4
The DTR*

This worksheet is designed to assist you in identifying your automatic thoughts. Noting your automatic thoughts can help you determine what underlying schemas or beliefs relate to particular events or situations. What are your automatic thoughts related to your relationships? For example, when you experience tension in your relationship, do you experience negative thoughts about yourself such as "I'll never succeed in a relationship"? Your therapist will help you with the rest.

Date/Time	Situation	Automatic thought	Emotion	Adaptive response	Outcome

*(Adapted from J. S. Beck, *Cognitive Therapy: Basics and Beyond*. Guilford Press, 1995©.)

WORKSHEET 5
Schemas

What are your rules or schemas related to relationships? Take a moment to write them down.

_____

_____

_____

_____

_____

_____

_____.

Choose any of these specific rules and fill in each of the columns. Indicate what the rule is, where (or whom) it comes from, what meaning it has for you, and how likely or easy it would be for you to change that rule. Once you have identified your particular schemas, how strong they are, and whether or not they can be changed, you can begin to create treatment goals.

Schema	Where it comes from	Meaning to me	Easy to change?

WORKSHEET 6
Treatment Goals

This worksheet asks you to identify your treatment goals, the symptoms that prevent you from obtaining your goals, the schemas that are associated with those goals, and the change for which you are hoping. Are you able to imagine yourself completing the goals? Complete this chart with the help of your therapist and prioritize the importance of each of these goals.

	Symptoms that prevent you from obtaining goal	Schema associated with goal	Hoped-for change	Realistic or unrealistic?	How outcome looks if goal is reached
Goal 1: **Highest priority**					
Goal 2: **High priority**					
Goal 3: **Moderate priority**					
Goal 4: **Low priority**					

Your therapist will help you complete this worksheet.

Date of Assessment: _____

FREEMAN DIAGNOSTIC PROFILING SYSTEM
(© FREEMAN, 2003) REVISED EDITION

Session#: _____ Evaluator: _____

Patient Name: _____ Patient#: _____ Location: _____

Birthdate: _____ Age: _____ Race: _____ Gender: _____ Birthorder: _____ Marital/Children: _____

Employment: _____ Education: _____ Disability: _____ Medication: _____

Physician: _____ Referral Question: _____

Instructions: Record the diagnosis including the code number. Briefly identify the criteria for the selected diagnosis. Working with the patient either directly as as part of the data gathering of the clinical interview, SCALE the SEVERITY of EACH CRITERION for the patient at the PRESENT TIME. Indicate the level of severity on the grid.

DIAGNOSIS (DSM/ICD) with Code:

Axis I: _____

Axis II: _____

Axis III: _____

SEVERITY OF SYMPTOMS — HIGH / MEDIUM / LOW (vertical scale 1–10)

DESCRIPTIVE CRITERIA (horizontal scale 0–12)

CRITERIA:

1 _____   7 _____

2 _____   8 _____

3 _____   9 _____

4 _____   10 _____

5 _____   11 _____

6 _____   12 _____

Do you believe that the above noted criteria are a reaonably accurate sample of the patient's behavior? **YES** or **NO**

If **NO**, please indicate why: _____

Are there any reasons to believe that this individual is an imminent danger to himself/herself or others? **YES** or **NO**

If **YES**, please indicate the danger: _____

(From Freeman, 1998.)

WORKSHEET 7
Physical Triggers

Physical sensations are clues to help you avoid future distressful situations. Your heart may have raced just before or during an argument with someone close to you. Perhaps your muscles tightened when you became upset. Your body might be giving you very strong messages. Think of the experience you described in WORKSHEET 2: THE ASSIGNMENT. What were you physically experiencing before, during, and after you had difficulty in an important relationship? You might have felt some of the following:

- queasy stomach.
- sweating/clammy skin.
- racing heart.
- tension.
- GI distress.

Use the lines below to describe your physical sensations.

_____

_____

_____

_____

_____

_____

_____

_____

_____

_____

_____

_____

_____

_____

_____

_____

WORKSHEET 8
Physical Triggers & Suggested Interventions

Three techniques can help you combat the physiological distress that occurs prior to, during, and/or after experiencing problems with relationships: (1) take a moment to stop; (2) employ relaxation techniques; and (3) use relaxing imagery.

Stop

In WORKSHEET 4, you identified the thoughts that directly related to your problems with relationships. For this exercise, identify the thoughts that seem to be creating or exacerbating uncomfortable physical reactions. Stopping is particularly important in relationships. As your reactions greatly influence your relationships, taking a moment to stop to regroup and curtail negative thoughts can be beneficial for both you and the other person. It gives you a chance to organize your thoughts, consider the consequences, and return to a relaxed state. When you are relaxed, you are better able to consider your next move. Use the lines below to write down the thoughts related to your physical reactions.

_____

_____

_____

_____

_____ .

As soon as you experience a thought that is related to your physical upset, stop what you are doing. Unpleasant thoughts often can get out of control. Like a runaway freight train, the thoughts gain momentum and speed and need to be stopped. You can do this by

_____

_____

_____

_____ .

Relax

In WORKSHEET 3, you identified what specific physical symptoms occur when you are having difficulty in your relationship. If you know what physical symptoms are related to problems in your relationship, use relaxation after you have taken a moment to stop. This can be as simple as just sitting down and taking a few deep breaths. For example, you might want to tell the person with whom you are having problems with that you just need a moment to regroup and relax. I can relax by

_____

_____

_____

_____ .

Use Relaxing Imagery

To help you continue relaxing, think of a safe place that you know makes you feel better. Your safe place might include being in the company of people with whom you feel safe and comfortable, and who would give you support if they were physically with you.

I feel safe imagining _____

_____

_____.

I hear _____

_____

_____.

I feel _____

_____

_____.

I can see _____

_____

_____.

I can smell _____

_____

_____.

I can taste _____

_____

_____.

My safe person who can join me here is _____

_____

_____.

WORKSHEET 9
Emotional Triggers

How would you describe the emotions you felt when you were having problems with your relationship? As relationships are important to all of us, they usually stir up very intense, sometimes even overwhelming, emotions. Use WORKSHEETS 3 AND 4 to identify some of the feelings you had when you were having problems with your relationships. They might include some of the following:

- fear.
- anger.
- sadness.
- disgust.

What were you feeling emotionally? Write down what those feelings were like.

_____

_____

_____

_____

_____

_____

_____

_____

_____

_____

_____

_____

_____

_____

_____

_____

_____

_____

_____

WORKSHEET 10
Emotional Triggers & Suggested Interventions

The following exercises are designed to help you with your emotions. Sometimes emotions become so powerful that decisions are made "from the heart," without thinking. These exercises can help you understand your emotions and how they can impact your decisions.

Scale Back

Relationships often trigger dramatic emotional responses. You might feel intense anger from feelings of rejection or fear, or you might feel incredible sadness. Try to turn your emotions down and scale back; It will help you feel more in control. Pick one of the uncomfortable emotional responses you wish to address from WORKSHEET 9. On a scale of 1 to 10 (1 being least severe and 10 being most severe), rate the severity of the emotion you experienced when you had difficulty in a relationship.

1   2   3   4   5   6   7   8   9   10

As you continue to have uncomfortable emotions related to relationships try to scale back or "turn the oven down." You might want to combine scaling back with some relaxation techniques described in WORKSHEET 8 on physical triggers. Once you have turned yourself down, rate your emotions again.

1   2   3   4   5   6   7   8   9   10

How did you do? Were you able to turn yourself down? You'll notice that with practice, turning down your own emotional temperature becomes easier and easier. Can you describe how you are feeling now?

_____

_____

_____

_____

_____

_____

Improve Communication of Feelings

Relationships require communication. It is vital that you express your emotions in such a way that the other person (the receiver) understands what you really mean. As trouble in a relationship is usually a result of problematic communication, let's examine how you send your messages to the other person.

How do you send your messages? Watch how you communicate nonverbally and verbally. Do you yell? Shake your fist?

What kind of messages do you send? Do you make statements that are condescending or that put the other person down? Do they relate to the issue at hand? Do you make negative statements about yourself?

How do you think the receiver perceives the messages? How do his or her responses contribute to your messages?

Do you ask if the other person understands your message? Do you prompt the other person to repeat what you just said in order to clarify?

The Communication Patterns Chart						
Sender of message	Receiver	Message	Verbal communication	Nonverbal communication	Type of communication (e.g., derogatory, self-deprecating)	Receiver's interpretation of message

Communication is very complicated and takes practice, but with time and energy you might find that your relationships improve, even when you have conflict, as each of you may learn to express yourself.

The following techniques can help you communicate and express your emotions in such a way that the other person can understand how you are feeling. See if these techniques change your interactions with others.

Use "I" Statements

Use "I" statements to express how you are feeling in the moment. Let the other person know what kinds of feelings you are having. When you stay with "I" statements there really can't be any confusion about who is feeling what.

I am feeling _____

_____ .

I am unsure if _____

_____ .

I _____

_____ .

Stay Cool

In relationships, we tend to have very strong emotions. Remember the scaling back exercise? Staying cool involves reminding yourself that you need to turn yourself down before reacting to the other person. The other person will perceive not only *what* you are saying but also *how* you are saying it. For example, even though you might want to convince the other person that you aren't angry, yelling that you aren't angry sends a confusing and contradictory message.

No Cursing Allowed

Vulgar statements only add fuel to an already smoldering fire. Others usually remember curses or crude things that are said to them, even if they were said in the "heat of the moment." By not cursing, you demonstrate that even though you may be hurt, afraid, or even angry, you respect others enough to not curse.

See What's Coming

Do you and another person have a typical way of arguing or resolving conflict? Are you able to see what's coming? If you can, you will be able to prepare yourself and maybe even break the cycle by changing your typical reactions.

I tend to resolve conflict by _____

_____

_____ .

My arguments with others usually end with me _____

_____

_____ .

My arguments with others usually end with them _____

_____

_____ .

I would like to change the way I resolve conflict by _____

_____

_____ .

Bridge the Gap

Is there room for compromise? Are you able to offer a compromise or help the other person come up with one? Have you both looked at ways to resolve the conflict?

I can compromise usually if _____

_____

_____ .

Times I am not able to compromise include _____

_____

_____ .

I would like to be able to compromise more about _____

_____

_____ .

See the Grays in Life

Is there something that you both might be missing? Is there something other than the two sides that you are both seeing or reacting to? What is the "gray" of the situation? This exercise is similar to the DICHOTOMOUS THINKING CHART that challenges black-and-white thinking.

The black of the situation is _____

_____

_____ .

The white of the situation is _____

_____

_____.

The grays of the situation are _____

_____

_____.

It Doesn't Have to End

Do you or the other person typically threaten to end the relationship when you are emotionally charged up? When you are in the heat of the moment, you might feel so overwhelmed with your emotions that you see no way out. By seeing the grays of the situation and promising yourself and the other person that you won't threaten to end or permanently change the relationship, you build a path toward better communication of your feelings. This communication comes out of clear thinking and is not based solely on intense emotions.

Take Turns

Are you letting the other person make his or her own "I" statements? Often miscommunication occurs because we don't hear each other or let the other person tell us how he or she is feeling. By stopping and allowing the other person to express him- or herself, you build a bridge to his or her perceptions and how your behaviors affect others.

I feel _____

_____

_____.

He or she feels _____

_____

_____.

I then say _____

_____

_____.

WORKSHEET 11
Cognitive/Automatic Thoughts

What thoughts were running through your mind before, during, and after you were having problems in your relationship? What main thoughts do you have about relationships? Are your thoughts related to how you feel about yourself as a result of relationship problems? Do you tend to jump to conclusions quickly? Refer to WORKSHEET 4: THE DTR to identify the specific thoughts related to this topic. Write your responses below.

_____

_____

_____

_____

_____

_____

_____

_____

_____

_____

_____

_____

_____

_____

_____

_____

_____

_____

_____

_____

_____

_____

WORKSHEET 12
Cognitive/Automatic Thoughts & Suggested Interventions

As you review WORKSHEET 4, you may notice some patterns in how you act in your relationships. Your automatic thoughts related to the relationship might be acting like a lit match on the kerosene of your emotions. The following interventions will help you control the thoughts that might be contributing to problems in your relationships.

Challenge Catastrophic Thinking

Do you tend to assume the worst? Challenge the catastrophic thoughts related to yourself, your significant other, and your relationship. Fill in the chart below, noting any catastrophic thought that is related to situations in which you encounter problems in your relationship. For instance, during an argument you might have the catastrophic thought that the relationship is automatically over. Then challenge yourself to identify the noncatastrophic thought related to having an argument. For example, disagreements often occur in relationships and they certainly don't always mean it is over.

The Catastrophic Thinking Chart		
Situation	**Catastrophic thought**	**Noncatastrophic thought**
_____ .	_____ .	_____ .
_____ .	_____ .	_____ .
_____ .	_____ .	_____ .
_____ .	_____ .	_____ .
_____ .	_____ .	_____ .
_____ .	_____ .	_____ .
_____ .	_____ .	_____ .
_____ .	_____ .	_____ .

Challenge Black-and-White Thinking

Are you thinking of your relationships only in terms of black and white? Do you have a hard time seeing the grays? For example, have you thought something like the following:

Your partner goes out ➔ *(means* only *that)* ➔ *you are being abandoned.*

Use your paint palette to mix the blacks and whites. What grays, or other options, are you able to come up with? For example, if your relationship is experiencing some conflict, does it automatically mean it is over? If your partner disappoints you, does it mean that he or she is all bad, without any good qualities? Challenge yourself to identify the grays. (Examples are provided to assist you.)

The Dichotomous Thinking Chart

Black   **Gray(s)**   **White**

|-----------------------------------|--------------------------------|-----------------------------------|

He's terrible.   *He's not always bad.*   *He's perfect.*

_____ .   _____ .   _____ .

_____ .   _____ .   _____ .

_____ .   _____ .   _____ .

_____ .   _____ .   _____ .

I have a hard time mixing grays related to _____

_____

_____

_____

_____

Weigh the Evidence

Try to prove yourself wrong. Often your erroneous conclusions lead you to behave in ways or say things you might later regret. Look at the most distressing conclusions you have drawn about events in your relationships and try to identify statements that contradict your conclusions. (Examples are provided to assist you.)

The Disputation Chart

Situation: *Argument with partner.*

Belief: *Partner won't love me.*

Proof Supporting Belief
1. *We argued.*
2. *Partner disagrees with me.*
3. _____ .
4. _____ .
5. _____ .
6. _____ .

Refuting Statement
1. *Conflict can help the relationship.*
2. *Can disagree and still love the other.*
3. _____ .
4. _____ .
5. _____ .
6. _____ .

WORKSHEET 13
Behavioral Triggers

What specific behaviors did you engage in before, during, and after you were having problems in your relationship? Relationships tend to bring out many emotions. You might have acted in ways you didn't intend because you felt overwhelmed with emotion. What things do you regret you did or wish you had done?

Before:

Behavior 1 _____.

Behavior 2 _____.

Behavior 3 _____.

During:

Behavior 1 _____.

Behavior 2 _____.

Behavior 3 _____.

After:

Behavior 1 _____.

Behavior 2 _____.

Behavior 3 _____.

Detail as much information regarding your behaviors as possible. Use the lines below.

_____

_____

_____

_____

_____

_____

_____

_____

_____

_____

WORKSHEET 14
Behavioral Triggers & Suggested Interventions

Scan the list you just made and identify which specific behaviors you wish to address.

Behavior 1 _____.

Behavior 2 _____.

Behavior 3 _____.

The following interventions can help you alter your behaviors in response to problems in your relationship.

Consider the Consequences

Before you act, consider the consequences to yourself, your partner, and the relationship. It may be hard to do, especially if you are in the heat of the moment, but stop and consider how your behaviors could affect things.

The Negative and Positive Consequences Chart		
Behavior	**Negative consequences**	**Positive consequences**
_____	_____	_____
_____	_____	_____
_____	_____	_____

After completing the chart, ask yourself the following:

- Do the negative consequences outweigh the positive consequences?
- Is it worth it to decrease this behavior?
- Do I want to continue this behavior?

Stop

Take a moment to stop. We all tend to experience physiological sensations in reaction to what we perceive. Once you recognize that you are experiencing that familiar physical sensation, take a moment to just stop. If you are having a thought like "Oh, no, my relationship is failing again," try to stop the thought. It might be helpful to imagine a stop sign or to snap a rubber band against your wrist.

Relax

If you have become very upset or have noticed that you are responding to intense feelings about your relationship, you might be experiencing agitation or anxiousness. This usually involves some physical reaction (e.g., stomach problems, a rapid heartbeat, and/or sweating). These types of feelings and bodily reactions respond well to relaxation techniques. Try breathing deeply and relaxing in a comfortable chair.

Use Relaxing Imagery

While you stop and relax your muscles, imagine your safe place. Where do you feel safe? Be sure to think of all of the aspects of your safe place. Because you may be feeling especially alone when you believe that someone is leaving you, you may want to imagine that a "safe person" such as a good friend or confidant is with you.

I feel safe imagining _____

_____

_____.

I hear _____

_____

_____.

I feel _____

_____

_____.

I can see _____

_____

_____.

I can smell _____

_____

_____.

I can taste _____

_____

_____.

My safe person who can join me here is _____

_____

_____.

WORKSHEET 16
Situational Triggers

There are times, individuals, events, and places that cause a great deal of distress. Knowing which situations cause you difficulty can help you be prepared if a similar situation occurs; in particular, you can be on alert for your alarms. You identified your four areas of warning signs in WORKSHEET 3: THE INCIDENT CHART. Now list the situations in which you have had problems with relationships. This might be when you are under extreme stress, have a limited amount of time, or feel you have felt slighted in some way. Review WORKSHEET 1 if you need help identifying these situations.

1. _____

_____

_____.

2. _____

_____

_____.

3. _____

_____

_____.

4. _____

_____

_____.

5. _____

_____

_____.

6. _____

_____

_____.

WORKSHEET 17
Situational Triggers & Suggested Interventions

WORKSHEET 16 identifies the situations in which you have experienced difficulty in relationships. Although not all situations or relationships are avoidable—for example, you may have to interact with work colleagues even if it causes distress—there are some situations that you can avoid. For those that are not avoidable you can choose to change your reactions. The following are brief descriptions of interventions that can be applied to any distressful situation.

Remove Yourself

Sometimes emotions become so overwhelming we that have trouble turning them down in the moment. If you feel as if you are not going to be able to stop yourself from doing something you really don't want to do, try taking a walk, go into another room, or let the other person know you need a few moments to "regroup" and remove yourself from the situation.

When things get particularly difficult, I can _____

_____

_____

_____

_____

_____

_____

_____.

Try Something Different

Is there something else you can try? What else could you do? For example, instead throwing something out of anger, could you go for a walk? Call a friend?

Instead of _____ [*behavior*],

I can try _____

_____

_____

_____

_____

_____

_____.

Your therapist will help you complete this worksheet.

Date of Assessment: _____

FREEMAN DIAGNOSTIC PROFILING SYSTEM

(© FREEMAN, 2003) REVISED EDITION

Session#: _____ Evaluator: _____

Patient Name: _____ Patient#: _____ Location: _____

Birthdate: _____ Age: _____ Race: _____ Gender: _____ Birthorder: _____ Marital/Children: _____

Employment: _____ Education: _____ Disability: _____ Medication: _____

Physician: _____ Referral Question: _____

Instructions: Record the diagnosis including the code number. Briefly identify the criteria for the selected diagnosis. Working with the patient either directly as as part of the data gathering of the clinical interview, SCALE the SEVERITY of EACH CRITERION for the patient at the PRESENT TIME. Indicate the level of severity on the grid.

DIAGNOSIS (DSM/ICD) with Code:

Axis I: _____

Axis II: _____

Axis III: _____

SEVERITY OF SYMPTOMS — HIGH / MEDIUM / LOW

DESCRIPTIVE CRITERIA

CRITERIA:

1 _____   7 _____

2 _____   8 _____

3 _____   9 _____

4 _____   10 _____

5 _____   11 _____

6 _____   12 _____

Do you believe that the above noted criteria are a reaonably accurate sample of the patient's behavior? **YES** or **NO**

If **NO**, please indicate why: _____

Are there any reasons to believe that this individual is an imminent danger to himself/herself or others? **YES** or **NO**

If **YES**, please indicate the danger: _____

(From Freeman, 1998.)

CHALLENGING WHAT YOU KNOW & DO: TAKING CONTROL

Relationships are a basic part of life. Every day we relate to ourselves and others. If you have experienced problems in your relationships, you might feel as if you will never be in a relationship that feels right. Relationships are patterns of interactions and responses. Once you have figured out your typical way of interacting, you can examine how your expectations, thoughts, hopes, and communication styles add to or detract from your relationships. By understanding your own patterns, you take steps toward improving not only your relationships themselves, but also how you feel about yourself as a partner in a relationship.

CHAPTER 3

Defining Yourself: Who Am I Anyway?

Everyone questions who he or she is. Throughout life we try on different hats to see which fits the best at a particular time; we try to find a role, set of values, occupation, or identity that feels right. We select ideals and values with which we are most comfortable. Over time these values and beliefs solidify into what we call *the self* or *identity*, that is, who we are to ourselves and who we appear to be to others. Our identity also separates us from those around us.

However, some of us have more difficulty selecting which things, values, and ways of behaving by which to identify ourselves. Even if we know that there are certain things we like and want to do, we might have problems merging them into a solid sense of self. Sometimes this difficulty can be related to our age, as our age, or maturity, changes throughout our lives. For example, peers are very important to teenagers; it is vital to a teen that he or she look a certain way, act and behave like peers, or even adopt the characteristics of some idealized figure. Sometimes the figure is someone they know like a relative. Other times it is a public figure, like a famous athlete; they may even don the same athletic wear worn by the athlete. Still other times the ideal person is a fantasy figure of their own creation.

We all, at times, try to identify ourselves by means of outside resources. Experimenting with new and different modes of appearance or behavior,

we take on, at least aspects of, different persons. We watch others and adapt. We might try new behaviors, change goals or occupations, or seek unfamiliar challenges or relationships. It can be something as simple as a new way of dressing; it could be a new haircut; it might mean moving to a new location; it could be getting a Harley Davidson motorcycle and a black leather jacket when we traditionally dressed "preppy." People might be shocked by our attempts to try on new images, behaviors, and personas. Questions might arise regarding our self-image or even our sexual orientation.

When we have trouble with our identity, nothing seems to fit just right. Those of us who have this difficulty are almost always in the "search mode." We often don't stop long enough to fully examine how well any individual identity fits. This endless searching leads to continuous questioning not only about who we are but about our purpose or the meaning of our live. If we are without a determinate purpose, we may feel bored, have low self-esteem, and believe that we don't belong to any one subculture, group, or niche. This may become a very powerful and painful disruption in our everyday existence.

We have a strong survival instinct to belong. Not feeling a part of something or not having a clearly defined self can add to feelings of loneliness or alienation. At times we react to these feelings by identifying very strongly with others. This might ease the discomfort for a little while. Sometimes we even strongly identify with those whom we have just met; this occurs because our own sense of self seems so vacant. The result? The rapid, unexpected changes in values and beliefs may confuse and worry family members and friends, and might ultimately lead us to things we normally wouldn't do.

Have you ever noticed that certain people you know seem very "together"? They are apparently able to say what they want, how they want it, and when they want it. And it isn't just a fluke; they're like that nearly all the time. Have you experienced times when you just don't know what you want or who you are? Whom you belong to? Or where you're going? Just like a child feels unsafe without structure, you might have experienced a sense of incompleteness or of "not being finished." You may have felt that you don't have an internal frame of reference. And as you develop into a full-fledged adult who, as society says, should know what you want and who you are, you might struggle to "keep up pretenses."

How does this happen? All of us are different. But some people who experience this ambiguous sense of self lacked structure as a child. For many reasons, structure helps a child feel safe. Ideally, though not always, it provides a much-needed safety net. Children who have this safety net know what to expect and when to expect it. This allows them to venture outward, with confidence, into the world. They experiment and get to know who they are as people. They consider different ideas about life, its events, and all of its complications.

When we experience trouble in the world, we maintain our balance by anchoring to something that appears solid. Hopefully that anchor is ourselves. However, those who didn't have a safety net during childhood might anchor anywhere; they don't necessarily seek refuge within themselves. Think of a ship crossing the ocean at night without the help of a compass. Heavy fog is blocking the view. Unsure of direction or course, the captain blindly continues forward, hoping to find a safe harbor in which to anchor. The place the captain finds may not be home port, but it's good enough for rest and repair. However, ultimately the port may not be completely right or the best place for the captain or the vessel to stay.

If you move through life without direction or a compass, you, too, might be continually anchoring at random harbors just to provide safety against the dangers of the deep waters or stresses of life's voyage. You may have noticed that you attach very quickly to others and immediately identify with them. If you do identify quickly with others, you tend to feel safer. You might change your clothing style, your everyday expressions, your activities, your choices of food or movies, and even where you live. This is usually all in an attempt to feel as if you belong, like you are part of a bigger plan or group. Although you initially may be satisfied with your new self, old worries and concerns eventually rear their ugly head. Your new lifestyle may not be compatible with your old, recurring patterns, and you may find that suddenly things don't feel as comfortable with this new arrangement of people, places, and activities.

In truth, you really do have some sense of yourself. It just has become difficult for you to recognize. You may have ideas about what you want or need, but you are unable to describe them. This chapter will help you identify your own safe harbor in which to anchor, so you can feel secure in the night and not seek temporary refuge in a foreign port.

VIGNETTES

Vignette 1: Marianne

There she goes again. A different hairstyle and color. The girls at the dorm wondered not only how Marianne could afford her frequent hair-dressing appointments, but also why she didn't get tired of changing so often.

Marianne looked at herself approvingly in the mirror. This bright pink color was just right for her; it fit in perfectly with the girls she had started hanging out with from a nearby college. They were really wild, and Marianne thought it was time to have more fun. Her friends here at school kept asking her to return all the things she had borrowed from them. She had no idea where their stuff was. She didn't even wear that stupid style anymore, and it just didn't matter; she was sick of them anyhow.

Vignette 2: Terry

Terry was in his early forties. He kept pushing the thoughts that he would never amount to anything to the back of his mind. Sure, most other men at his age had homes, families, and careers. He just hadn't figured out what he wanted yet. He'd attended a community college for a year when he was 19, but he just didn't fit in with that crowd. The school . . . well he just couldn't get into that scene. He would try a job for a few weeks and then, bored with the work, quit. His friends seemed to change along with his jobs; not to mention his girlfriends. They changed all too often as well. How is a guy supposed to figure out what to do or what he wants? "Oh well," he thought, "by the time I figure it out, it'll be time to retire!"

Review the Vignettes

Do either of these individuals sound familiar to you? Have you felt that you were more likely to adapt your style to new groups of people because you felt you really didn't have a style of your own? Everyone recasts their self, to a certain extent, in order to fit in. We all follow rules of custom and law, such as not talking in a library or stopping at a red light. But there is plenty of room for individual differences. You might have noticed, however, that you tend to adopt patterns or styles that match the people with whom you are currently socializing. You might have even changed some of your long-term plans or long-held beliefs in order to fit in.

WHAT YOU WOULD LIKE TO CHANGE

First, discuss with your therapist whether this seems to be an area that is problematic for you. Do you relate to the vignettes? Does this behavior appear to occur as a pattern? Is it an area of your life over which you wish you had more control? If it does not seem pertinent, discuss with your therapist whether you need to continue to the assessment section.

SELF-MONITORING: HOW DO I KNOW WHAT MY PERCEPTIONS ARE?

How can you enhance your sense of identity? You can by learning more about yourself—what you like, what you don't like, and, most importantly, discover the things that really do define you as unique. Understanding how you perceive yourself is a vital part of understanding who you are and what your identity is. You might have been ignoring bodily, emotional, cognitive, and behavioral signs that could help you better understand yourself. The goal is to try to heighten your perceptions regarding your likes and dislikes and the signs that help define your identity.

THE WORKSHEETS

The following section includes several worksheets that address the current chapter topic. The worksheets are designed to help you learn more about yourself so that you can decide if there is anything you wish to change. You therapist can help you use them.

WORKSHEET 1
The Assessment

Rate the severity of the following problems as you think they may relate to you.

0 = none   1 = mild   2 = moderate   3 = severe   4 = extremely severe

1. You frequently change groups of friends.   ____

2. You have tried many types of careers and still feel unsatisfied.   ____

3. You are not sure what your self-image is.   ____

4. You have questioned your sexual orientation on more than one occasion.   ____

5. You have surprised family and/or friends by changing long-held values.   ____

6. You have found it difficult to maintain employment for any length of time.   ____

7. You tend to forget about friends you've known for a long time to hang around new friends.   ____

8. Your taste in clothes, style, and activities frequently changes.   ____

9. In order to fit in you're willing to "go with the crowd" even if it entails doing something you are hesitant about.   ____

10. You tend to get bored very easily.   ____

If you rated several of these items as representing the way you think or feel, you might lack a sense of belonging to or participation in some group or endeavor. Being a part of something helps us identify who and what we are.

WORKSHEET 2
The Assignment

Think of a time when you felt as if you had no idea what your identity was. You might have questioned your own purpose, motives, or direction. This caused you great distress. Often these feelings can be precipitated by stress. Stress can lead you to define yourself by becoming involved in something that you don't really want to be a part of. Use the lines below to detail your experience. Be as specific as possible. You will compile your reactions in WORKSHEET 3: THE INCIDENT CHART.

_____

_____

_____

_____

_____

_____

_____

_____

_____

_____

_____

_____

_____

_____

_____

_____

_____

_____

_____

_____

_____

WORKSHEET 3
The Incident Chart*

This worksheet will help you begin uncovering the schemas related to this characteristic. Think about the situation you described in WORKSHEET 2 and ask yourself the following:

- What was I physically experiencing before, during, and after the situation?
- What was I feeling?
- What thoughts were running through my mind before, during, and after the situation?
- How was I behaving? [*name some specific behaviors*]

Now fill out the worksheet in as much detail as possible.

Situation: _____

_____.

Prior to Incident

Physiological sensations	Emotions	Cognitions/ thoughts	Behaviors
_____.	_____.	_____.	_____.
_____.	_____.	_____.	_____.
_____.	_____.	_____.	_____.
_____.	_____.	_____.	_____.

During Incident

Physiological sensations	Emotions	Cognitions/ thoughts	Behaviors
_____.	_____.	_____.	_____.
_____.	_____.	_____.	_____.
_____.	_____.	_____.	_____.
_____.	_____.	_____.	_____.

After Incident

Physiological sensations	Emotions	Cognitions/ thoughts	Behaviors
_____.	_____.	_____.	_____.
_____.	_____.	_____.	_____.
_____.	_____.	_____.	_____.
_____.	_____.	_____.	_____.

*(Adapted from J. S. Beck, *Cognitive Therapy: Basics and Beyond.* Guilford Press, 1995©.)

WORKSHEET 4
The DTR*

This worksheet is designed to assist you in identifying your automatic thoughts. Noting your automatic thoughts can help you determine what underlying schemas or beliefs relate to particular events or situations. What are your automatic thoughts related to how you define yourself? For example, when you are attempting to make a decision, do you experience thoughts such as "Why can't I ever know what I really want?" or "Because I never know what I want, I am worthless"?

Date/Time	Situation	Automatic thought	Emotion	Adaptive response	Outcome

*(Adapted from J. S. Beck, *Cognitive Therapy: Basics and Beyond*. Guilford Press, 1995©.)

WORKSHEET 5
Schemas

What are your rules or schemas related to your identity? Take a moment to write them down.

_____

_____

_____

_____

_____

_____

_____ .

Choose any of these specific rules and fill in each of the columns. Indicate what the rule is, where (or whom) it comes from, what meaning it has for you, and how likely or easy it would be for you to change that rule. Once you have identified your particular schemas, how strong they are, and whether or not they can be changed, you can begin to create treatment goals

Schema	Where it comes from	Meaning to me	Easy to change?

WORKSHEET 6
Treatment Goals

This worksheet asks you to identify your treatment goals, the symptoms that prevent you from obtaining your goals, the schemas that are associated with those goals, and the change for which you are hoping. Are you able to imagine yourself completing the goals? Complete this chart with the help of your therapist and prioritize the importance of each of these goals.

	Symptoms that prevent you from obtaining goal	Schema associated with goal	Hoped-for change	Realistic or unrealistic?	How outcome looks if goal is reached
Goal 1: Highest priority					
Goal 2: High priority					
Goal 3: Moderate priority					
Goal 4: Low priority					

Your therapist will help you complete this worksheet.

FREEMAN DIAGNOSTIC PROFILING SYSTEM
(© FREEMAN, 2003) REVISED EDITION

Date of Assessment: _____

Session#: _____ Evaluator: _____

Patient Name: _____ Patient#: _____ Location: _____

Birthdate: _____ Age: _____ Race: _____ Gender: _____ Birthorder: _____ Marital/Children: _____

Employment: _____ Education: _____ Disability: _____ Medication: _____

Physician: _____ Referral Question: _____

Instructions: Record the diagnosis including the code number. Briefly identify the criteria for the selected diagnosis. Working with the patient either directly as as part of the data gathering of the clinical interview, SCALE the SEVERITY of EACH CRITERION for the patient at the PRESENT TIME. Indicate the level of severity on the grid.

DIAGNOSIS (DSM/ICD) with Code:

Axis I: _____

Axis II: _____

Axis III: _____

SEVERITY OF SYMPTOMS / HIGH / MEDIUM / LOW

DESCRIPTIVE CRITERIA

CRITERIA:

1 _____   7 _____

2 _____   8 _____

3 _____   9 _____

4 _____   10 _____

5 _____   11 _____

6 _____   12 _____

Do you believe that the above noted criteria are a reaonably accurate sample of the patient's behavior? **YES** or **NO**

If **NO**, please indicate why: _____

Are there any reasons to believe that this individual is an imminent danger to himself/herself or others? **YES** or **NO**

If **YES**, please indicate the danger: _____

(From Freeman, 1998.)

WORKSHEET 7
Physical Triggers

Physical sensations are clues to help you avoid future situations in which you perceive that you have difficulty defining who you are. They might be very strong messages from your body (e.g., a pounding heart, stomach problems, or a general tenseness in your muscles). Think of the experience you described in WORKSHEET 2: THE ASSIGNMENT. What were you physically experiencing before, during, and after you perceived you were without direction or were lost? You might have felt some of the following:

- queasy stomach.
- sweating/clammy skin.
- racing heart.
- tension.
- GI distress.

Use the lines below to describe your physical sensations.

_____

_____

_____

_____

_____

_____

_____

_____

_____

_____

_____

_____

_____

_____

_____

WORKSHEET 8
Physical Triggers & Suggested Interventions

Three techniques can help you combat the physiological distress that occurs prior to, during, and/or after experiencing a lack of a sense of self or identity: (1) take a moment to stop; (2) employ relaxation techniques; and (3) use relaxing imagery.

Stop

If you notice your system turning itself up when you become convinced that you are alone and have no idea who you are, take a moment to stop. For this exercise, identify the thoughts that seem to be creating or exacerbating uncomfortable physical reactions. Use the lines below to write down those thoughts.

_____

_____

_____

_____

As soon as you experience a thought that is related to your physical upset, stop what you are doing. Unpleasant thoughts often can get out of control. Remind yourself that there are unique aspects about yourself. Reflect upon those unique qualities and stop. You can do this by

_____

_____

_____

_____

Relax

When you relax, you are reinforcing your individuality; you are taking control by accessing your own body and its response system. Answer the following questions in order to determine how your unique system works.

When I am able to relax I notice my muscles _____

_____

When I am able to relax I notice my body _____

_____

When I am able to relax I notice my breathing _____

_____

When I am able to relax I notice my heart rate _____

_____

I have trouble relaxing when _____

_____.

Now that you are aware of how your body relaxes or becomes tense, you can use this information to inform yourself when to use relaxation techniques and exercises.

Relaxing Imagery

Your safe place is just that—yours. You have identified something that is safe for you and only you. Use these thoughts to help you relax and stay centered.

I feel safe imagining _____

_____

_____.

I hear _____

_____

_____.

I feel _____

_____

_____.

I can see _____

_____

_____.

I can smell _____

_____

_____.

I can taste _____

_____

_____.

My safe person who can join me here is _____

_____

_____.

WORKSHEET 9
Emotional Triggers

How would you describe the emotions you experienced when you felt you didn't belong or were lost? Use WORKSHEETS 3 and 4 to identify some of the feelings you had when you felt you didn't belong or were lost. They might include some of the following:

- fear.
- anger.
- sadness.
- disgust.

What were you feeling emotionally? Write down what those feelings were like.

_____

_____

_____

_____

_____

_____

_____

_____

_____

_____

_____

_____

_____

_____

_____

_____

_____

_____

WORKSHEET 10
Emotional Triggers & Suggested Interventions

Feeling as if you do not fit or are unable to define yourself can prompt very intense emotions. At times, it can even trigger impulsivity and lead you to do things you might later regret. Not understanding who you are can also lead you to become swayed by the group you are in. Do you feel sadness? Anger? Envy?

Scale Back

Pick one of the uncomfortable emotional responses you wish to address from WORKSHEET 9. On a scale of 1 to 10 (1 being least severe and 10 being most severe), rate the severity of the emotion you experienced when you questioned your identity or felt lost.

1	2	3	4	5	6	7	8	9	10

As you continue to have uncomfortable emotions related to your identity or feeling lost, try to scale back or "turn the oven down." You might want to combine scaling back with some relaxation techniques described in WORKSHEET 8 on physical triggers. Once you have turned yourself down, rate your emotions again.

1	2	3	4	5	6	7	8	9	10

How did you do? Were you able to turn yourself down? You'll notice that with practice, turning down your own emotional temperature becomes easier and easier. Can you describe how you are feeling now?

_____

_____

_____

_____

_____

_____

_____

_____

_____

_____

_____

_____

_____

WORKSHEET 11
Cognitive/Automatic Thoughts

What thoughts were running through your mind before, during, and after you felt alone, without direction, or lacking an identity? Did you experience thoughts related to being confused? Alone? Misunderstood? Did you not know how to make the next move in life or did you not trust yourself to do it? Your thoughts could have included negative self-statements or statements about how you wish you could be more like others. Refer to WORKSHEET 4: THE DTR to identify the specific thoughts related to this topic. Write your responses below.

_____

_____

_____

_____

_____

_____

_____

_____

_____

_____

_____

_____

_____

_____

_____

_____

_____

_____

_____

_____

WORKSHEET 12
Cognitive/Automatic Thoughts & Suggested Interventions

Most of the following tasks include some form of self-monitoring. The exercises will help you not only understand who and what you are but also actually progress in learning to define aspects of yourself. The goal is for you to define your anchor, or that place in yourself that will always be there and upon which you can always rely. Instead of scaling back, cognitively *turn up* your perceptions about what makes you unique.

Intervention 1

To begin with, describe yourself. Write anything that comes to mind. Imagine trying to describe yourself to someone you have never met using as few words as possible. Who are you?

_____

_____

_____

_____

_____

_____

Did you have trouble doing this? You might find that the next exercise helps.

Intervention 2

Review the following list marking an "x" next to the items that apply to you and filling in the blanks for those items.

sex	_____	sexual orientation	_____	daughter/son	_____
occupation	_____	political affiliation	_____	neighbor	_____
race	_____	hair color	_____	student	_____
age	_____	clothing style	_____	parent	_____
ethnicity	_____	height	_____	brother/sister	_____
citizenship	_____	city of origin	_____	other	_____
religion	_____	urban/suburban	_____		
marital status	_____	friend	_____		

By filling in the prompts above, you are beginning to create a working self-concept. Looking at the above list, you can begin to see all of the varying aspects of your unique self, your identity.

Intervention 3

Now rank how much you identify with each item on a scale of 1 to 5, with 1 being "not identifying strongly" and 5 being "identifying very strongly." (For example, if Philadelphia is your city of origin, how much do you identify yourself as a Philadelphian?) It may help to compare the various categories. (For example, do you think of yourself more as a teacher than as a friend?) Don't get caught up in value judgments such as "It's better to be a friend than a teacher".

sex	____	sexual orientation	____	daughter/son	____
occupation	____	political affiliation	____	neighbor	____
race	____	hair color	____	student	____
age	____	clothing style	____	parent	____
ethnicity	____	height	____	brother/sister	____
citizenship	____	city of origin	____	other	____
religion	____	urban/suburban	____		
marital status	____	friend	____		

Now you have a template for who you are. For example, a single mother raising four children alone will probably rank her identity as a parent as greater than that of a neighbor. By having the clear identity of *parent*, she has a role-specific self-concept in society. Her role as a parent is vital to her children's existence. She behaves as a parent, thinks as a parent, and plans as a parent. What are your roles? How have you defined yourself?

Intervention 4

Take a moment to examine how you identified yourself. Now try combining the various aspects of your identity. For example, the mother raising her children alone might write: "I am a single parent living in Philadelphia." With the combination of these three categories (i.e., marital status, parental status, city of residence) we can begin to paint a picture of who this woman is and what she may be like. We may also begin to speculate about what is important for her. Try this exercise for yourself. You may strongly identify yourself with your occupation, or as a friend, or as a male or female. There are no right or wrong answers. Use the following sentence to help you:

I am a _____-year-old _____ [*sex*] living in _____ [*city*].

What does this information tell you? That as a _____-year-old living in _____, you probably are drawn to certain types of activities, certain places to shop, particular types of music and food, and perhaps a specific type of neighborhood. Much of this information is consistent, and you can rely upon it when you're feeling lost. You are establishing your anchor. Now try other combinations:

I am a _____ who likes and identifies with _____.

I am a _____ who likes and identifies with _____.

Intervention 5

Weigh the evidence. Use the DISPUTATION CHART to try to prove or disprove your beliefs that you don't have an identity by creating refuting statements that contradict your beliefs. (Examples are provided to assist you.)

The Disputation Chart

Situation: *Having difficulty contributing to conversation.*

Belief: *I have nothing to contribute.*

Proof Supporting Belief

1. *I have no idea who I am.*
2. *I don't ever know what to say.*

3. _____ .

4. _____ .

5. _____ .

6. _____ .

Refuting Statement

1. *I know that I am _____ [use list].*
2. *I have a history and unique experiences that others might find interesting.*

3. _____ .

4. _____ .

5. _____ .

6. _____ .

Remember this chart during those times when you feel you have no identity, don't fit in, or are lost.

WORKSHEET 13
Behavioral Triggers

What specific behaviors did you engage in before, during, and after you felt you didn't belong or were unsure of who you were? Did you find yourself changing your plans to suit others? Perhaps you changed your attitude about something like politics or personal styles. Maybe you have pulled away from social situations because you felt as if you had nothing to contribute. How did you handle these painful feelings?

Before:

Behavior 1 _____.

Behavior 2 _____.

Behavior 3 _____.

During:

Behavior 1 _____.

Behavior 2 _____.

Behavior 3 _____.

After:

Behavior 1 _____.

Behavior 2 _____.

Behavior 3 _____.

Detail as much information regarding your behaviors as possible. Use the lines below.

_____

_____

_____

_____

_____

_____

_____

_____

_____

_____

WORKSHEET 14
Behavioral Triggers & Suggested Interventions

Scan the list you just made and identify which specific behaviors you wish to address.

Behavior 1 _____.

Behavior 2 _____.

Behavior 3 _____.

The following interventions that can help alter your behaviors in response to feeling like you don't belong or being unsure of who you are.

Consider the Consequences

Before you act, consider the consequences of your behaviors. For example, if you are feeling like you need to follow others because you are unsure of what you want at the moment, consider what would happen if you did what others are doing. Now consider the opposite: waiting to figure out what you really want. With time, what you want will become apparent.

The Negative and Positive Consequences Chart		
Behavior	**Negative consequences**	**Positive consequences**
_____	_____	_____
_____	_____	_____
_____	_____	_____
_____	_____	_____
_____	_____	_____
_____	_____	_____
_____	_____	_____
_____	_____	_____

After completing the chart, ask yourself the following:

- Do the negative consequences outweigh the positive consequences?
- Is it worth it to decrease this behavior?
- Do I want to continue this behavior?

WORKSHEET 16
Situational Triggers

There may be times, individuals, events, and places that cause a great deal of distress. Knowing which situations cause you difficulty can help you be prepared if a similar situation occurs; in particular, you can be on alert for your alarms. You identified your four areas of warning signs in WORKSHEET 3: THE INCIDENT CHART. Now list situations in which you tend to feel alone, are without a sense of purpose or direction, or think that you can't identify yourself. Is it when you are with your friends? Family? When you are in public or talking to someone who is an authority figure? perhaps when you are at a party with many people you don't know? Review WORKSHEET 1 if you need help identifying these situations.

1. _____

_____

_____.

2. _____

_____

_____.

3. _____

_____

_____.

4. _____

_____

_____.

5. _____

_____

_____.

6. _____

_____

_____.

WORKSHEET 17
Situational Triggers & Suggested Interventions

Worksheet 16 identifies the situations in which you have felt alone, without a sense of purpose or direction, or as if you can't identify yourself. Although not all situations are avoidable that cause distress, there are some situations that you can avoid. For those that are not avoidable, you can choose to change your reactions. The following are brief descriptions of interventions that can be applied to any distressful situation.

Remove Yourself

If you find yourself in a situation where you have become overwhelmed with feelings of incompetence, you can choose to remove yourself from this type of situation. In this way, you can take charge of the situation, and feel more in control that you are making your own decision to leave.

When things get particularly difficult, I can _____

_____

_____

_____

_____

_____

_____.

Try Something Different

Is there something else you can try? What else could you do? You might want to try a new behavior or situation without committing yourself to it until you find what feels right for you. Sometimes when we are in a social situation we may feel pressured to try what everyone else is trying. You might go with the crowd even though it doesn't feel right.

Instead of _____ [*behavior*],

I can try _____

_____

_____

_____

_____

_____

_____.

The DPS

Your therapist will help you complete this worksheet.

Date of Assessment: _____

FREEMAN DIAGNOSTIC PROFILING SYSTEM
(© FREEMAN, 2003) REVISED EDITION

Session#: _____ Evaluator: _____

Patient Name: _____ Patient#: _____ Location: _____

Birthdate: _____ Age: _____ Race: _____ Gender: _____ Birthorder: _____ Marital/Children: _____

Employment: _____ Education: _____ Disability: _____ Medication: _____

Physician: _____ Referral Question: _____

Instructions: Record the diagnosis including the code number. Briefly identify the criteria for the selected diagnosis. Working with the patient either directly as as part of the data gathering of the clinical interview, SCALE the SEVERITY of EACH CRITERION for the patient at the PRESENT TIME. Indicate the level of severity on the grid.

DIAGNOSIS (DSM/ICD) with Code:

Axis I: _____

Axis II: _____

Axis III: _____

SEVERITY OF SYMPTOMS — HIGH / MEDIUM / LOW

DESCRIPTIVE CRITERIA

CRITERIA:

1 _____ 7 _____

2 _____ 8 _____

3 _____ 9 _____

4 _____ 10 _____

5 _____ 11 _____

6 _____ 12 _____

Do you believe that the above noted criteria are a reaonably accurate sample of the patient's behavior? **YES** or **NO**

If **NO**, please indicate why: _____

Are there any reasons to believe that this individual is an imminent danger to himself/herself or others? **YES** or **NO**

If **YES**, please indicate the danger: _____

(From Freeman, 1998.)

CHALLENGING WHAT YOU KNOW & DO: TAKING CONTROL

You have taken the first step in challenging the belief that you don't know your identity. By identifying your unique alarm systems, you are defining how your own system reacts to stress. No one else has the combination of physical, emotional, cognitive, and behavioral reactions that you do. With this knowledge, you are armed to combat those negative and upsetting thoughts and beliefs. This will help you learn that you *are* unique.

CHAPTER 4

Do You Look Before You Leap? Reducing Risks

As children we are spontaneous creatures; we react to our surroundings with curiosity, attraction, and fear. As adolescents we continue to interact with the environment, including physical sensations (whether they are immediate or long-lasting). For example, we might react to the butterflies in our stomach when we meet someone we are attracted to, or we might react to feeling anxious or scared for long periods of time by doing something impulsive like lashing out at someone. As we mature, we learn when, where, and how to respond. Many of these lessons involve making sure that our responses are acceptable to society.

We might have learned from previous experience that acting on a whim can lead to something exciting, enjoyable, or pleasurable. However, we could have also learned that not looking before we leap can get us into trouble. Acting impulsively is often the result of being overaroused or excited, and not having a good outlet to appropriately channel this energy. To be impulsive is to sense an urge to do something and to act on the urge without careful consideration. These urges can be emotional (how we feel), physical (how our bodies respond), cognitive (how we think), or behavioral (how we act). Careful consideration can typically protect us from danger, damage, difficulty, or discomfort.

Some of us, however, have difficulty learning to consider the consequences of being spontaneous or impulsive. We might have chosen to do something dangerous, like driving too fast, because our friends were "egging us on"; because of that peer pressure we failed to consider the dangers of high-speed driving, getting into legal trouble, damaging or harming your car, or, worse, placing lives at risk. We might be impulsive by jumping into a relationship very quickly or by trying a drug without considering the potential dangers. If you tend to be impulsive, friends perhaps have described you as liking "the wild side," and you might have paid the price for your wild behavior on more than one occasion for your actions. Do you look before you leap?

VIGNETTES

Vignette 1: Karen

Karen was frustrated with work. She felt tired, underappreciated, and she was annoyed with her supervisor. She really didn't feel like working the rest of the day; she had the urge to just walk out. So when her girlfriends called to ask her out, she readily accepted. Without much thought, she concluded that the company owed her some hours because she had been working so hard recently. She straightened her desk quickly, set her phone to voicemail, and left 2 hours early. She was shocked when she received her termination notice the following day.

Vignette 2: Jenny

Jenny had been waiting for this party all week. Her girlfriends told her there would be lots of great-looking guys. She had had such bad luck with men lately. She couldn't seem to find "the one." She took extra time getting ready and was sure to wear something sexy. When she arrived, she loosened up with a few drinks. She didn't want to appear stiff or stuffy. Then it happened. She met the man of her dreams. He was great-looking, talented, and with a great job; they talked together so easily. The night flew. He just seemed to know her. They told each other their innermost secrets; she never had felt this close to anyone before. Before long, she found herself at his apartment. She knew it was going too fast, but she was sure he was the one. His wife, however, tended to disagree.

Review the Vignettes

Do either of these individuals sound like you? Do you tend to act on impulses? Both of the characters had impulses and made a conscious choice to act on them. Everyone in life has spontaneous moments; however, the characters' spontaneous actions caused negative consequences they later regretted. Your impulsiveness might not be as dramatic as the forms of impulsiveness featured in the vignettes. But perhaps you have noticed that you tend not to look before you leap.

WHAT YOU WOULD LIKE TO CHANGE

First, discuss with your therapist whether this seems to be an area that is problematic for you. Do you relate to the vignettes? Does this behavior appear to occur in a pattern? Is it an area of your life over which you wish you had more control? If it does not seem pertinent, discuss with your therapist whether you need to continue to the assessment section.

SELF MONITORING: HOW DO I KNOW WHAT MY PERCEPTIONS ARE?

If you have identified that you might be impulsive, the first and foremost question you must ask yourself before you act on an impulse is: *What do I want to accomplish by doing this act?* As discussed previously, some impulsive behaviors can lead to rewarding circumstances; other impulsive behaviors, however, don't. It's important to remember that although some behaviors contain some enjoyment, the level of danger associated with the negative consequence might outweigh any positive feelings. It is imperative, therefore, that you learn to identify your warning signs in order to prevent yourself from acting impulsively.

People who are impulsive tend to disregard their alarm system and ignore their warning signs. They could even feel as if they don't have any warning signs at all. But there is always some sort of event, trigger, or flag to indicate that you might be about to act impulsively. Although being spontaneous can be fun, we need to carefully weigh how we react in situations that could land us in trouble. To help you learn about your impulses, try to recognize the perceptions that lead to your becoming impulsive.

THE WORKSHEETS

The following section includes several worksheets that address the current chapter topic. The worksheets are designed to help you learn more about yourself so that you can decide if there is anything you wish to change. Your therapist can help you use them.

WORKSHEET 1
The Assessment

Rate the severity of the following problems as you think they may relate to you. If you aware of any other impulsive behaviors that you do that are not included on the list, please add them.

0 = none   1 = mild   2 = moderate   3 = severe   4 = extremely severe

1. I drink to excess or am unable to stop. ____

2. I use drugs to excess or am unable to stop. ____

3. I engage in sexual relations without adequately protecting myself or that place me in danger. ____

4. I place myself in dangerous situations, such as driving too fast or frequenting dangerous areas. ____

5. I run up bills that I know I am unable to pay for. ____

6. I eat excessively, knowing that it may make me feel bad. ____

7. I yell at others without first trying to resolve the situation quietly. ____

8. I miss school/work for reasons other than sickness. ____

9. I throw objects. ____

10. I physically fight with others. ____

If you rated several of these items as representing the way you often behave, you might be considered impulsive.

WORKSHEET 2
The Assignment

Think of a time where you acted impulsively. You might have done something, said something, or found your-self in a situation that you later regretted. You perhaps have heard yourself saying, "I can't believe I did that" or "Next time I'll think twice." Use the lines below to detail your experience. Be as specific as possible. You will compile your reactions in WORKSHEET 3: THE INCIDENT CHART.

_____

_____

_____

_____

_____

_____

_____

_____

_____

_____

_____

_____

_____

_____

_____

_____

_____

_____

_____

_____

WORKSHEET 3
The Incident Chart*

This worksheet will help you begin uncovering the schemas related to this characteristic. Think about the situation you described in WORKSHEET 2 and ask yourself the following:

- What was I physically experiencing before, during, and after the situation?
- What was I feeling?
- What thoughts were running through my mind before, during, and after the situation?
- How was I behaving? [*name some specific behaviors*]

Now fill out the worksheet in as much detail as possible.

Situation: _____

_____

Prior to Incident

Physiological sensations	Emotions	Cognitions/ thoughts	Behaviors
_____	_____	_____	_____
_____	_____	_____	_____
_____	_____	_____	_____
_____	_____	_____	_____

During Incident

Physiological sensations	Emotions	Cognitions/ thoughts	Behaviors
_____	_____	_____	_____
_____	_____	_____	_____
_____	_____	_____	_____
_____	_____	_____	_____

After Incident

Physiological sensations	Emotions	Cognitions/ thoughts	Behaviors
_____	_____	_____	_____
_____	_____	_____	_____
_____	_____	_____	_____

*(Adapted from J. S. Beck, *Cognitive Therapy: Basics and Beyond.* Guilford Press, 1995©.)

WORKSHEET 4
The DTR*

This worksheet is designed to assist you in identifying your automatic thoughts. Noting your automatic thoughts can help you determine what underlying schemas or beliefs relate to particular events or situations. What are your automatic thoughts related to your impulsivity? Do you experience thoughts such as "If I can't do what I want when I want, will I not be able to have fun"? Your therapist will help you with the rest.

Date/Time	Situation	Automatic thought	Emotion	Adaptive response	Outcome

*(Adapted from J. S. Beck, *Cognitive Therapy: Basics and Beyond.* Guilford Press, 1995©.)

WORKSHEET 5
Schemas

What are your rules or schemas related to being impulsive? Take a moment to write them down.

_____

_____

_____

_____

_____

_____

_____.

Choose any of the specific rules and fill in each of the columns. Indicate what the rule is, where (or whom) it comes from, what meaning it has for you, and how likely or easy it would be for you to change that rule. Once you have identified your particular schemas, how strong they are, and whether or not they can be changed, you can begin to create treatment goals.

Schema	Where it comes from	Meaning to me	Easy to change?

WORKSHEET 6
Treatment Goals

This worksheet asks you to identify your treatment goals, the symptoms that prevent you from obtaining your goals, the schemas that are associated with those goals, and the change that you are hoping for. Are you able to imagine yourself completing the goals? Complete this chart with the help of your therapist and prioritize the importance of each of these goals.

	Symptoms that prevent you from obtaining goal	Schema associated with goal	Hoped-for change	Realistic or unrealistic?	How outcome looks if goal is reached
Goal 1: **Highest priority**					
Goal 2: **High priority**					
Goal 3: **Moderate priority**					
Goal 4: **Low priority**					

The DPS

Your therapist will help you complete this worksheet.

Date of Assessment: _____

FREEMAN DIAGNOSTIC PROFILING SYSTEM
(© FREEMAN, 2003) REVISED EDITION

Session#: _____ Evaluator: _____

Patient Name: _____ Patient#: _____ Location: _____

Birthdate: _____ Age: _____ Race: _____ Gender: _____ Birthorder: _____ Marital/Children: _____

Employment: _____ Education: _____ Disability: _____ Medication: _____

Physician: _____ Referral Question: _____

Instructions: Record the diagnosis including the code number. Briefly identify the criteria for the selected diagnosis. Working with the patient either directly as as part of the data gathering of the clinical interview, SCALE the SEVERITY of EACH CRITERION for the patient at the PRESENT TIME. Indicate the level of severity on the grid.

DIAGNOSIS (DSM/ICD) with Code:

Axis I: _____

Axis II: _____

Axis III: _____

SEVERITY OF SYMPTOMS

DESCRIPTIVE CRITERIA

CRITERIA:

1 _____   7 _____

2 _____   8 _____

3 _____   9 _____

4 _____   10 _____

5 _____   11 _____

6 _____   12 _____

Do you believe that the above noted criteria are a reaonably accurate sample of the patient's behavior? **YES** or **NO**

If **NO**, please indicate why: _____

Are there any reasons to believe that this individual is an imminent danger to himself/herself or others? **YES** or **NO**

If **YES**, please indicate the danger: _____

(From Freeman, 1998.)

WORKSHEET 7
Physical Triggers

Physical sensations are clues to help you avoid future situations that could have negative consequences. Think of the experience you described in WORKSHEET 2: THE ASSIGNMENT. What were you physically experiencing before, during, and after you were impulsive? Your physical experiences might not necessarily feel uncomfortable; sometimes they indicate your excitement about something. You might have felt some of the following:

- queasy stomach.
- sweating/clammy skin.
- racing heart.
- tension.
- GI distress.

Use the lines below to describe your physical sensations.

_____

_____

_____

_____

_____

_____

_____

_____

_____

_____

_____

_____

_____

_____

_____

WORKSHEET 8
Physical Triggers & Suggested Interventions

Physical indicators and warning signs can be our only signal when we are about to become impulsive. Again, these need not be negative signs; they often are signs of excitement or anticipation. By taking into consideration where these physical sensations (pleasant or unpleasant) could lead you, you are in effect making a conscious decision about how you want to act rather than being a victim of your own impulses. Three techniques can help you combat the physiological arousal that leads to impulsivity: (1) take a moment to stop; (2) employ relaxation techniques; and (3) use relaxing imagery.

Stop

Stopping is particularly important when managing physical signs that indicate that you might act impulsively. Although you want to pursue or continue with a good feeling, take a moment to stop. For this exercise, identify the thoughts that seem to be creating or exacerbating physical reactions. Use the lines below to write down those thoughts.

_____

_____

_____

_____

_____.

As soon as you experience a thought that is related to your physical reactions, stop what you are doing. Allow your mind to catch up with your beating heart! You can do this by

_____

_____

_____

_____.

Relax

In WORKSHEET 3, you identified what specific physical symptoms occur when you are impulsive. If you know what physical symptoms are related to impulsivity, use relaxation after you have taken a moment to stop. This can be as simple as just sitting down and relaxing. Take a few deep breaths when you note that you are becoming overexcited or responding physically to things around you that may lead you to be impulsive. I can relax by

_____

_____

_____

_____.

Relaxing Imagery

Imagine a relaxing scene that includes you relaxing after you've realized that you've stopped yourself from doing something you would have regretted.

I feel safe imagining _____

_____

_____.

I hear _____

_____

_____.

I feel _____

_____

_____.

I can see _____

_____

_____.

I can smell _____

_____

_____.

I can taste _____

_____

_____.

My safe person who can join me here is _____

_____

_____.

WORKSHEET 9
Emotional Triggers

How would you describe the emotions you had when you were about to be impulsive? Are you most impulsive when you are feeling really happy? Very angry? What usually happens is that when we become very impulsive, we don't give our heads a chance to catch up to our emotions. In other words, we "think" with our heart rather than with our head. Use WORKSHEETS 3 and 4 to identify some of the feelings you had when you felt impulsive. They might include some of the following:

- fear.
- anger.
- sadness.
- disgust.

What were you feeling emotionally? Write down what those feelings were like.

_____

_____

_____

_____

_____

_____

_____

_____

_____

_____

_____

_____

_____

_____

_____

_____

WORKSHEET 10
Emotional Triggers & Suggested Interventions

Feelings of both a negative and positive nature can lead to impulsivity. Perhaps you felt sad or gloomy, and believed that you deserved something more. Or perhaps you were "taken with a moment of passion" and acted on impulse. As with most problem areas, scaling back those emotions can help you avoid acting impulsively.

Scale Back

Pick one of the emotional responses you wish to address from WORKSHEET 9. On a scale of 1 to 10 (1 being least severe and 10 being most severe), rate the severity of the emotion or urge that you experienced when you were impulsive.

1   2   3   4   5   6   7   8   9   10

As you continue to have emotions related to being impulsive, try to scale back or "turn the oven down." You might want to combine scaling back with some relaxation techniques described in WORKSHEET 8 on physical triggers. Once you have turned yourself down, rate your emotions again.

1   2   3   4   5   6   7   8   9   10

How did you do? Were you able to turn yourself down? You'll notice that with practice, turning down your own emotional temperature becomes easier and easier. Can you describe how you are feeling now?

_____

_____

_____

_____

_____

_____

_____

_____

_____

_____

_____

_____

_____

Attach Emotion to Impulsiveness

Learn to attach your experienced emotion with pending impulsivity. In other words, if you know from WORK-SHEET 3: THE INCIDENT CHART that you tend to act on your urges when you are sad, you can begin to set up some safeguards for yourself when you are sad. For example, someone might attach emotions to his impulsiveness by stating: "When I am psyched and wound up, I tend to act impulsively, especially when I'm out with the guys." Keep your own patterns in mind.

In the past, I have reacted strongly to _____ [*emotion*].

When I feel _____ , I tend to act impulsively.

I have trouble controlling my impulses when _____

_____

_____

_____

_____ .

Learn to Identify When You're Feeling Vulnerable

At times you probably have noticed that if you are feeling slightly more vulnerable, you tend to get yourself into trouble by acting on impulse. Is it when you are tired? When you feel rejected? Bored? Perhaps if you drink alcohol? List the times when your vulnerability leads to impulsiveness.

I know I am vulnerable during _____

_____

_____

_____

_____ .

I know I am vulnerable when _____

_____

_____

_____

_____ .

I am especially vulnerable at _____ times in my life.

WORKSHEET 11
Cognitive/Automatic Thoughts

What thoughts were running through your mind before, during, and after you were impulsive? Were you able to identify them? Often when we are impulsive, we haven't thought! However, there is always a brief moment when you consider whether or not to act. What happens in your mind then? Are there thoughts that include "It won't hurt anybody" or "Everyone needs to have a little fun" or "I'll worry about this tomorrow?" It may be hard, but try to capture those thoughts that rush through your mind before, during, and after you do something impulsive. Refer to WORKSHEET 4: THE DTR to identify the specific thoughts related to this topic. Write your responses below.

_____

_____

_____

_____

_____

_____

_____

_____

_____

_____

_____

_____

_____

_____

_____

_____

_____

_____

_____

_____.

WORKSHEET 12
Cognitive/Automatic Thoughts & Suggested Interventions

In order to understand impulsivity, it is important to recognize the role cognition plays in handling or not handling impulses or urges. In order to decrease your impulsivity, it is vital that you be able to read the physical and emotional warning signs (listed in WORKSHEET 3) that you might be about to engage in impulsive behavior. If you can read those signs, you can use your thought processes to make decisions about how you want to act. The negative consequences of not looking before you leap are usually connected to not giving your mind a chance to catch up.

Consider the Consequences

Plug in the impulsive behaviors that you want to alter and the potential negative and positive consequences of those behaviors. (Examples are provided to assist you.)

The Catastrophic Thinking Chart		
Situation *Accepting a ride from an attractive stranger.*	**Catastrophic thought** *Potential danger.*	**Noncatastrophic thought** *Excitement.*

After completing the chart, ask yourself the following:

• Do the negative consequences outweigh the positive consequences?
• Is it worth it to decrease this behavior?
• Do I want to continue this behavior?

By connecting the physical, emotional, and situational triggers that generally have led you to be impulsive, you allow your mind to catch up. This will allow you to make an informed decision. That means you have made a step toward taking control, as you now are making a choice, *your* choice.

Avert Impulsivity

Complete the IMPULSIVITY CHART (Pretzer, 1990) and review the following five steps to learn how you can take control of your impulses and make more informed decisions about behaviors that have both long- and short-term effects on your life.

Impulsivity Chart*

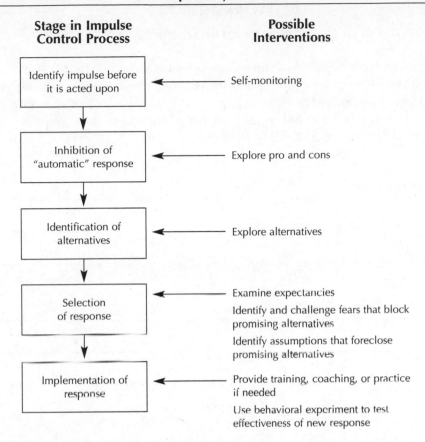

| Stage in Impulse Control Process | Possible Interventions |

*(From J. Pretzer [1990]. Borderline personality disorder. In A. Beck, A. Freeman, & Associates [eds.], *Cognitive therapy of personality disorders* [pp. 176–207]. New York: Guilford Press. Reprinted by permission of the Guilford Press.)

1. *Identify the impulse.* What is the urge?
2. *Inhibit the automatic responses.* What are the positives and negatives of acting upon a certain urge or impulse? How does it weigh out?
3. *Identify the options.* Explore. What are the alternatives to the behavior you wish to stop?
4. *Select a response.* Identify and challenge your fears related to alternatives. How do you make the choice to act or not to act? What are your expectations and hopes regarding the act or carrying out the urge?
5. *Implement a response.* Now make an actual choice about what you are going to do.

WORKSHEET 13
Behavioral Triggers

What specific behaviors did you engage in before, during, and after you were impulsive? This is a particularly important area to consider when looking at impulsivity. You might have said something you regret. You could have done something that got you into trouble legally, at work, or even with friends or significant others. Perhaps you have consumed too much alcohol or used drugs that led you to do even more regrettable behaviors. It might almost be painful to remember them!

Before:

Behavior 1 _____ .

Behavior 2 _____ .

Behavior 3 _____ .

During:

Behavior 1 _____ .

Behavior 2 _____ .

Behavior 3 _____ .

After:

Behavior 1 _____ .

Behavior 2 _____ .

Behavior 3 _____ .

Detail as much information regarding your behaviors as possible. Use the lines below.

_____

_____

_____

_____

_____

_____

_____

_____

_____

_____

_____ .

WORKSHEET 14
Behavioral Triggers & Suggested Interventions

Scan the list you just made and identify which specific behaviors you wish to address.

Behavior 1 _____.

Behavior 2 _____.

Behavior 3 _____.

The following interventions can help you alter your behaviors in response to feeling an urge to be impulsive.

Avoid the Situation

Avoid the situations you have identified as leading to impulsive behaviors. (Avoiding them completely might not always be possible.)

When I'm starting to feel impulsive, I can go _____

_____

_____.

Identify a Friend

Call or contact your safe person to help you manage your impulses.

When I want to do something I may regret, I can call/contact _____

_____

_____.

Consider Triggers

The substance-abuse field has a well-known mantra: "Avoid people, places, and things associated with your addiction." There are patterns pertaining to when and where you tend to act on urges. Try to identify and list these triggers clearly, so that when they appear, you can recognize that you are heading into a situation that could result in impulsive behavior.

Play "What If" Games

Ask yourself: "What if I did this? What if I didn't?" Or, if you are remembering something you already did, ask yourself: "What would have happened if I hadn't done that?"

Reward Yourself

Reward yourself when you resist acting on an impulse.

I can reward myself by _____

_____

_____.

WORKSHEET 16
Situational Triggers

There are times, individuals, events, and places that trigger your impulsivity. Knowing which situations cause you difficulty can help you be prepared if a similar situation occurs; in particular, you can be on alert for your alarms. You identified your four areas of warning signs in WORKSHEET 3: THE INCIDENT CHART. Now list the situations in which you tend to be impulsive. You might be able to identify certain times of the week, people you are around, or different types of venues (e.g., restaurants, bars) in which you tend to be more impulsive. Review WORKSHEET 1 if you need help identifying these situations.

1. _____

_____

_____.

2. _____

_____

_____.

3. _____

_____

_____.

4. _____

_____

_____.

5. _____

_____

_____.

6. _____

_____

_____.

WORKSHEET 17
Situational Triggers & Suggested Interventions

WORKSHEET 16 identifies those situations in which you have become impulsive. If you are in a situation similar to or included in that list, the following interventions can help you avoid doing something impulsive.

Remove Yourself

If you find yourself in a situation where you have become impulsive, remember that you can choose to remove yourself from the environment which could stimulate impulsive acts. By choosing to remove yourself from a situation known to result in impulsive acts, you can take charge of the situation.

When things get particularly difficult, I can _____

_____

_____

_____

_____

_____

_____

_____.

Try Something Different

What actions can you take instead of acting on an impulse? Perhaps you believe that if you don't act on an urge, you'll be considered boring or dull. However, there are alternatives to acting impulsively (e.g., planning an event that can provide as much enjoyment as acting on an urge does). A second component of this intervention is to identify and create other activities. Create a list of activities you can do instead of acting on an impulse, and create a plan for carrying out these behaviors. For example, if you like to exercise, daily runs could be included on your list.

Instead of _____ [*behavior*],

I can try _____

_____

_____

_____

_____

_____

_____.

The DPS

Your therapist will help you complete this worksheet.

Date of Assessment: _____

FREEMAN DIAGNOSTIC PROFILING SYSTEM
(© FREEMAN, 2003) REVISED EDITION

Session#: _____ Evaluator: _____

Patient Name: _____ Patient#: _____ Location: _____

Birthdate: _____ Age: _____ Race: _____ Gender: _____ Birthorder: _____ Marital/Children: _____

Employment: _____ Education: _____ Disability: _____ Medication: _____

Physician: _____ Referral Question: _____

Instructions: Record the diagnosis including the code number. Briefly identify the criteria for the selected diagnosis. Working with the patient either directly as as part of the data gathering of the clinical interview, SCALE the SEVERITY of EACH CRITERION for the patient at the PRESENT TIME. Indicate the level of severity on the grid.

DIAGNOSIS (DSM/ICD) with Code:

Axis I: _____

Axis II: _____

Axis III: _____

DESCRIPTIVE CRITERIA

CRITERIA:

1 _____   7 _____

2 _____   8 _____

3 _____   9 _____

4 _____   10 _____

5 _____   11 _____

6 _____   12 _____

Do you believe that the above noted criteria are a reaonably accurate sample of the patient's behavior? **YES** or **NO**

If **NO**, please indicate why: _____

Are there any reasons to believe that this individual is an imminent danger to himself/herself or others? **YES** or **NO**

If **YES**, please indicate the danger: _____

(From Freeman, 1998.)

CHALLENGING WHAT YOU KNOW & DO: TAKING CONTROL

Being aware that you have the tendency to be impulsive is half the battle. By just knowing that certain places or situations trigger impulsive behavior, you can employ various exercises to take control and change the outcome. You don't have to be someone who is always playing "Monday morning quarterback" and saying you should have done something in a different way or that you wish you had done something differently. You can be a person who can get an idea, an urge, or feel like you want to do something and, before you react, consider the consequences both for yourself and others around you. Then you can make your own decision about what to do. You are not just a product of urges and instincts!

CHAPTER 5 | Self-Injury: An Unnecessary Solution

This chapter addresses a common but very unnecessary aspect of being a sensitive person. Some people choose an unconventional means of helping themselves. This includes choosing to end their lives or to harm themselves to achieve some sort of relief. This book examines these two behaviors separately, although in real life they sometimes overlap. Suicide is the actual act of attempting to end one's life. Self-injurious behaviors are acts that are done when someone is overwhelmed with anxiety, extreme stress, and frustration or may lead to suicidal thinking.

If you recently considered either of these acts or have attempted to carry out these behaviors, you should seek psychological help immediately. Sometimes in life we become very depressed and feel as if there is just no way out. As you are a sensitive person, each and every stressor can feel like an unmanageable burden. During these times, you might actually become hopeless and despair of there being any possibility of change. You may view life, and all of its potential, as cloaked in darkness. Enveloped in this darkness, your feelings of hopelessness can lead to thoughts of death.

We all consider our own death and our own mortality. But when our thoughts lead us to consider taking our own lives, we must seek out alternate ways of taking care of ourselves; we must choose a way that is not irreversible. Our feelings of hopelessness act like a dark filter transforming and distorting all that we see. We might be unable to see the opportunity or potential for change, or feel powerless to enact it. We can believe that "ending it all" will enable us to no longer feel pain, or to avoid punishing our loved ones any more than we feel we already have. Death, however, is not the only solution; in fact, it is the worst choice among a number of negative choices.

Some data may help you choose options other than suicide or self-harm. They are offered as reminders of the long-lasting and devastating effects of suicide.

Suicide leads to familial depression; that is, it can have a very negative effect on families, children, and friends. They will all experience a sense of loss, as will members of your community.

Suicide is permanent; it leaves many options and paths what may have taken unexplored. Think of your family, and if you have children, understand the legacy that you will bestow upon them if you choose to take your life.

Suicide cannot be a means of revenge; if your choice of suicide is motivated by the desire to punish others for things they did or not do, to hurt them—forget it. If they were so unfeeling, uncaring, unyielding, and unloving, your death will probably be only an inconvenience or emotional speed bump along the road of their lives.

Self-mutilating or self-damaging acts are behaviors that inflict physical harm but may or may not be motivated by the intent to end one's life. These behaviors include anything that actually causes harm—e.g., acting recklessly, cutting or burning oneself, engaging in dangerous sexual situations, using drugs or alcohol, or knowingly placing oneself in any situation that could cause harm. It is often difficult for outsiders to understand why people hurt themselves. Often those who feel overwhelmed or anxious seek ways of reducing frustration, stress, or pain. Unable to find an outlet for these waves of intense emotion, some choose to harm themselves in order to divert the energy outside of their selves. In some cases the self-harm doesn't even cause pain, because the relief the individual feels after releasing the pent-up emotions is so great. However, long-term reminders are found in scarring, permanent injuries, harm to others, and even accidental death.

VIGNETTES

Vignette 1: Sherri

Sherri hated the mornings. While everyone else in the world was waking to the new day, showering, and preparing themselves for work, Sherri lay in bed, unsure, frightened, alone, and worst of all, convinced that things were never going to change. Losing her job 6 months ago was the last straw. Her husband Bob left her to live with his brother in a tiny one-bedroom apartment and said he would never come back. She must be really bad if he did that. Now she had no one. Sure, her friends said they cared, but they didn't really understand. She felt hopeless and was overwhelmed by her loneliness, her failures, her fears, and the horrible emptiness. She felt she no longer wanted to feel that pain anymore. She wanted to disappear. She went into the bathroom, poured a glass of water, and swallowed all of her medication.

Vignette 2: Kristy

Kristy was pacing in her apartment. She couldn't stand this feeling of panic and fear. Her therapist called it anxiety. Well, whatever it was, she wished it would just go away. She felt her hands shaking,

her heart pounding, and her stomach twisted in knots. She picked up a steak knife sitting on the kitchen table. As she was fidgeting with it, she scratched her arm with it. She stared at the small trickles of blood oozing from her arm and fixated on the rate of the drops falling to the floor. She seemed to feel calmer. She was letting the pain go, drop by drop, to the floor. She decided to try cutting herself again, this time on the other arm in a place where no one could see the mark it left.

Review the Vignettes

Do either of these situations seem to apply to you? Sometimes it is very difficult to acknowledge that you may be experiencing these very distressful symptoms. In both vignettes, the characters experienced overwhelming, intense emotions. Additionally, both felt they were unable to handle their emotions and, due to their feelings of helplessness, chose to harm themselves.

WHAT YOU WOULD LIKE TO CHANGE

This may be a difficult assessment for you to complete. It is especially important for you to be completely honest and for you to communicate your responses to your therapist. In this way, we can ensure that you are helped during these very difficult times.

SELF MONITORING: HOW DO I KNOW WHAT MY PERCEPTIONS ARE?

To begin with, you must learn to identify not only when you are experiencing urges to harm yourself, but also the situations that occur directly before you experience those impulses. In other words, you must learn to identify the triggers—the aspects of yourself and the environment that lead you on a course of self-destruction. Identifying changes in yourself in order to control them is not always an easy task. However, once you have mastered the ability to recognize not only the situations that lead you to harm yourself but also your own internal warning system, you can gain a sense of control over these thoughts and actions. This level of control also allows you to seek help.

If, as children, we learned that when things are really difficult the only way to help ourselves is to hurt ourselves, as adults we can continue this pattern by engaging in self-injurious behavior when stressors become overwhelming. Again, the key to taking control is learning when your alarm-system is triggered by an "intruder." An intruder can be anxiety, stressful situations, fighting with loved ones, or feeling overwhelmed and overburdened. If, however, you can identify when your triggers are activated, you can then choose your response. You can choose to call in the troops to help you *before* the intruder actually breaks in. In other words, you can seek assistance from both yourself and others when you become overwhelmed and before you actually act on the impulse to harm yourself.

THE WORKSHEETS

The following section includes several worksheets that address the current chapter topic. The worksheets are designed to help you learn more about yourself so that you can decide if there is anything you wish to change. Your therapist can help you use them.

WORKSHEET 1
The Assessment (Suicide)

Rate the severity of the following problems as you think they may relate to you.

0 = none	1 = mild	2 = moderate	3 = severe	4 = extremely severe

1. I have thoughts of dying.   ____

2. I have attempted to kill myself in the past.   ____

3. I have active thoughts of killing myself.   ____

4. I feel hopeless that life will never get better for me.   ____

5. Everything seems dark and cloudy for me.   ____

6. I think everyone would be better off without me.   ____

7. I have active plans to kill myself.   ____

8. No one understands how sad I really am.   ____

9. I wish I were never born.   ____

10. Death is a better option than the pain I feel.   ____

Often it is very difficult even to admit that you've had some of these ideas or have engaged in some of these acts. However, honesty is the first step in taking control of your life. In order to take control, you must be able to define and identify the problem. Your therapist will help you with these questions.

WORKSHEET 1
The Assessment (Self-Harm)

Rate the severity of the following problems as you think they may relate to you.

0 = none   1 = mild   2 = moderate   3 = severe   4 = extremely severe

1. I have intense waves of emotion or anxiety. ____

2. I have cut or burned myself in the past. ____

3. I do things that put me in harm's way. ____

4. I seem to get myself into trouble more than I should. ____

5. I sometimes pick at myself until I bleed. ____

6. I see no way to feel better other than to harm myself when I feel anxious. ____

7. I experience physical discomfort when I become upset (e.g., upset stomach, numbness, and difficulty breathing). ____

8. I think that the only way to relieve pain is to create it. ____

9. I feel I have little to no control over my actions. ____

10. If I start to harm myself I have difficulty stopping it. ____

Often it is very difficult even to admit that you've had some of these ideas or have engaged in some of these acts. However, honesty is the first step in taking control of your life. In order to take control, you must be able to define and identify the problem. Again, once the problem is defined, avenues for help and treatment become available. It's not possible to solve a puzzle without all of the pieces. However, when all of the pieces are available we can formulate a way to solve the puzzle and activate our plan to success. Your therapist will help you with these questions.

WORKSHEET 2
The Assignment

With the aid of your therapist, sit back, relax, and take three deep breaths through your nose. While you're beginning to relax, think of a time you wanted either to end your life or harm yourself in an attempt to make yourself feel better. These times might be difficult to recall, but we need the data from your experience to learn how you, in your own unique way, manage under stress. Use the lines below to detail your experience. Be as specific as possible. You will compile your reactions in WORKSHEET 3: THE INCIDENT CHART.

_____

_____

_____

_____

_____

_____

_____

_____

_____

_____

_____

_____

_____

_____

_____

_____

_____

_____

_____

_____

_____

_____

WORKSHEET 3
The Incident Chart*

This worksheet will help you begin uncovering the schemas related to this characteristic. Think about the situation you described in WORKSHEET 2 and ask yourself the following:

- What was I physically experiencing before, during, and after the situation?
- What was I feeling?
- What thoughts were running through my mind before, during, and after the situation?
- How was I behaving? [*name some specific behaviors*]

Now fill out the worksheet in as much detail as possible.

Situation: _____

_____.

Prior to Incident

Physiological sensations	Emotions	Cognitions/ thoughts	Behaviors
_____.	_____.	_____.	_____.
_____.	_____.	_____.	_____.
_____.	_____.	_____.	_____.
_____.	_____.	_____.	_____.

During Incident

Physiological sensations	Emotions	Cognitions/ thoughts	Behaviors
_____.	_____.	_____.	_____.
_____.	_____.	_____.	_____.
_____.	_____.	_____.	_____.
_____.	_____.	_____.	_____.

After Incident

Physiological sensations	Emotions	Cognitions/ thoughts	Behaviors
_____.	_____.	_____.	_____.
_____.	_____.	_____.	_____.
_____.	_____.	_____.	_____.

*(Adapted from J. S. Beck, *Cognitive Therapy: Basics and Beyond*. Guilford Press, 1995©.)

WORKSHEET 4
The DTR*

This worksheet is designed to assist you in identifying your automatic thoughts. Noting your automatic thoughts can help you determine what underlying schemas or beliefs relate to particular events or situations. What are your automatic thoughts related to harming yourself or attempting suicide? Do your thoughts include "I have little to live for" or "There's no way out"? Your therapist will help you with the rest.

Date/Time	Situation	Automatic thought	Emotion	Adaptive response	Outcome

*(Adapted from J. S. Beck, *Cognitive Therapy: Basics and Beyond.* Guilford Press, 1995©.)

WORKSHEET 5
Schemas

What are your rules or schemas related to suicidal or self-harming behaviors? Take a moment to write them down.

_____

_____

_____

_____

_____

_____.

Choose any of the specific rules and fill in each of the columns. Indicate what the rule is, where (or whom) it comes from, what meaning it has for you, and how likely or easy it would be for you to change that rule. Once you have identified your particular schemas, how strong they are, and whether or not they can be changed, you can begin to create treatment goals.

Schema	Where it comes from	Meaning to me	Easy to change?

WORKSHEET 6
Treatment Goals

This worksheet asks you to identify your treatment goals, the symptoms that prevent you from obtaining your goal, the schemas that are associated with those goals, and the change that you are hoping for. Are you able to imagine yourself completing the goals? Complete this chart with the help of your therapist and prioritize the importance of each of these goals.

	Symptoms that prevent you from obtaining goal	Schema associated with goal	Hoped-for change	Realistic or unrealistic?	How outcome looks if goal is reached
Goal 1: **Highest priority**					
Goal 2: **High priority**					
Goal 3: **Moderate priority**					
Goal 4: **Low priority**					

Your therapist will help you complete this worksheet.

Date of Assessment: _____

FREEMAN DIAGNOSTIC PROFILING SYSTEM
(© FREEMAN, 2003) REVISED EDITION

Session#: _____ Evaluator: _____

Patient Name: _____ Patient#: _____ Location: _____

Birthdate: _____ Age: _____ Race: _____ Gender: _____ Birthorder: _____ Marital/Children: _____

Employment: _____ Education: _____ Disability: _____ Medication: _____

Physician: _____ Referral Question: _____

Instructions: Record the diagnosis including the code number. Briefly identify the criteria for the selected diagnosis. Working with the patient either directly as as part of the data gathering of the clinical interview, SCALE the SEVERITY of EACH CRITERION for the patient at the PRESENT TIME. Indicate the level of severity on the grid.

DIAGNOSIS (DSM/ICD) with Code:

Axis I: _____

Axis II: _____

Axis III: _____

SEVERITY OF SYMPTOMS

HIGH / MEDIUM / LOW

DESCRIPTIVE CRITERIA

CRITERIA:

1 _____   7 _____

2 _____   8 _____

3 _____   9 _____

4 _____   10 _____

5 _____   11 _____

6 _____   12 _____

Do you believe that the above noted criteria are a reaonably accurate sample of the patient's behavior? **YES** or **NO**

If **NO**, please indicate why: _____

Are there any reasons to believe that this individual is an imminent danger to himself/herself or others? **YES** or **NO**

If **YES**, please indicate the danger: _____

(From Freeman, 1998.)

WORKSHEET 7
Physical Triggers

Physical sensations are clues to help you avoid future distressful situations. Think of the experience you described in WORKSHEET 2: THE ASSIGNMENT. What were you physically experiencing before, during, and after you had self-destructive impulses? Often intense arousal or anxiety accompanies the urge to harm oneself. If you were suicidal, you might have felt an intense lack of energy or slowness in your body. You might have felt some of the following:

- queasy stomach.
- sweating/clammy skin.
- racing heart.
- tension.
- GI distress.

Use the lines below to describe your physical sensations.

_____

_____

_____

_____

_____

_____

_____

_____

_____

_____

_____

_____

_____

_____

_____

_____

_____

_____

WORKSHEET 8
Physical Triggers & Suggested Interventions

From your list of physical responses, you can identify how your system attempts to manage stress through bodily channels. You can use those physical signs to help you reduce your discomfort when they are occurring, and as a warning that you could be reaching the point where you will want to harm yourself.

Three techniques can help you combat physiological distress: (1) take a moment to stop; (2) employ relaxation techniques; and (3) use relaxing imagery.

Stop

In WORKSHEET 4, you identified the thoughts directly related to self-harm. For this exercise, identify the thoughts that seem to be creating or exacerbating uncomfortable physical reactions. Use the lines below to write down those thoughts.

_____

_____

_____

_____

_____.

As soon as you experience a thought that is related to your physical upset that may lead to self-harm, stop what you are doing. Again, physical sensations can be very strong. They can lead you to act in ways you might later regret. There are many other things that you can do to experience relief or change the way you are feeling.

You can do this by _____

_____

_____

_____

_____.

Relax

In WORKSHEET 3, you identified what specific physical symptoms occur when you might harm yourself. If you know what physical symptoms are related to self-harm, you can utilize relaxation techniques when you experience those symptoms. Try to relax all of your muscles. Care for and nurture your body. Take extra care of yourself.

You can do this by _____

_____

_____

_____.

Relaxing Imagery

Relaxing imagery can be especially helpful when you are experiencing intense physical sensations. Use your safe person in your safe place to help protect you from self-harm. Imagine yourself not only getting through a very stressful time, but feeling good that you did not harm yourself.

I feel safe imagining _____

_____

_____.

I hear _____

_____

_____.

I feel _____

_____

_____.

I can see _____

_____

_____.

I can smell _____

_____

_____.

I can taste _____

_____

_____.

My safe person who can join me here is _____

_____

_____.

WORKSHEET 9
Emotional Triggers

How would you describe the emotions you had when you wanted to harm yourself? Often a sense of hopelessness or a feeling that you can't affect anything accompanies these impulses. You might have felt incredible sadness or complete emptiness. Use WORKSHEETS 3 and 4 to identify some of the feelings you had when you wanted to harm yourself. They might include some of the following:

- fear.
- anger.
- sadness.
- disgust.

What were you feeling emotionally? Write down what those feelings were like.

_____

_____

_____

_____

_____

_____

_____

_____

_____

_____

_____

_____

_____

_____

_____

_____

_____

_____

WORKSHEET 10
Emotional Triggers & Suggested Interventions

Feelings of desperation, anger, helplessness, and hopelessness often accompany urges to self-harm. In order to stop the cycle of hurting yourself, is imperative that you learn to identify which particular emotions trigger your urge to self-harm.

Scale Back

Pick one of the uncomfortable emotional responses you wish to address from WORKSHEET 9. On a scale of 1 to 10 (1 being least severe and 10 being most severe), rate the severity of the emotion you experienced when you felt the urge to harm yourself or end your life.

1   2   3   4   5   6   7   8   9   10

As you continue to have uncomfortable emotions related to self-harm, try to scale back or "turn the oven down." You might want to combine scaling back with some relaxation techniques described in WORKSHEET 8 on physical triggers. Once you have turned yourself down, rate your emotions again.

1   2   3   4   5   6   7   8   9   10

How did you do? Were you able to turn yourself down? You'll notice that with practice, turning down your own emotional temperature becomes easier and easier. Can you describe how you are feeling now?

_____

_____

_____

_____

_____

_____.

Attach Emotion to Self-Harm

Try to identify and attach your experienced emotion to pending self-harm. In other words, if you know from your list in WORKSHEET 3: THE INCIDENT CHART that you tend to act on your self-injurious urges when you are sad, you can begin to set up some safeguards for yourself when you are sad.

When I feel _____, I want to harm myself.

In the past, I have reacted strongly to _____ [*emotion*].

I have trouble controlling my urge to harm myself when _____

_____

_____

_____.

Learn to Identify When You're Feeling Vulnerable

At times you might have noticed that if you are feeling slightly more vulnerable, you tend to experience thoughts of self-harm. Try to list the times when your vulnerability leads to self-harm.

I know I am vulnerable during _____

_____

_____

_____ .

I know I am vulnerable when _____

_____

_____

_____ .

I am especially vulnerable at _____ during my life.

Challenge Feelings of Hopelessness

Hopelessness is a feeling often experienced by those who want to harm themselves. It is a bleak emotion that makes people feel as if there is nothing for them, ever. However, this emotion tends to wax, wane, and change. To combat these feelings, keep yourself armed with a list of times in your life when you were able to feel joy and happiness. This list can reinforce the fact that you are capable of having other emotions besides hopelessness. It is also a good idea to carry around a picture of a loved one and look at the picture when you feel overwhelmed and want to hurt yourself.

When I feel hopeless I can:

• Look at a picture of someone I care about.
• Think of family and friends.
• Know I've felt better before and can again.
• Give myself a chance to feel good again.
• Remember that I may have felt helpless before and managed to feel better again.
• Know that the future has options that are good for me.

• Other options: _____

_____

_____

_____

_____

_____ .

WORKSHEET 11
Cognitive/Automatic Thoughts

What thoughts were running through your mind before, during, and after you wanted to harm yourself? You might have felt hopeless and thought that you had no options other than self-harm. These thoughts are particularly important to identify. Once you know what particular thoughts set the self-harming process in motion, you can give yourself a chance to get the support you need at times when you have considered self-harm. Refer to WORKSHEET 4: THE DTR to help identify the specific thoughts related to this topic. Write your responses below.

_____

_____

_____

_____

_____

_____

_____

_____

_____

_____

_____

_____

_____

_____

_____

_____

_____

_____

_____

WORKSHEET 12
Cognitive/Automatic Thoughts & Suggested Interventions

Research has shown that hopelessness is a major predictor of completed suicides (Beck, 1986). What were you thinking prior to wanting to harm yourself? Did you think you lacked direction or control over life's events? Did you catastrophize events? In other words, do others describe you as someone who "makes a mountain out of a molehill"? Do you think in terms of black and white, where things seem either fantastic or horrendous? Often these extreme thoughts lead to feelings of hopelessness.

Challenge Catastrophic Thinking

Challenge the specific catastrophic thoughts that lead you to thoughts of self-harm. For example, if you have experienced a loss, are experiencing deepening stress, or feel hopeless, you may have the catastrophic thought "life will never get better." Challenge yourself to identify a competing noncatastrophic thought, such as "There will be better times or days."

The Catastrophic Thinking Chart		
Situation	**Catastrophic thought**	**Noncatastrophic thought**
_____	_____	_____
_____	_____	_____
_____	_____	_____
_____	_____	_____

Challenge Black-and-White Thinking

Consider the grays of the situation. (Examples are provided to assist you.)

The Dichotomous Thinking Chart		
Black	**Gray(s)**	**White**
I feel hopeless. I have no control.	I can take some control and relax and seek support from someone I trust.	My only option is to hurt or harm myself.
_____	_____	_____
_____	_____	_____
_____	_____	_____
_____	_____	_____

Weigh the Evidence

Challenge yourself to produce evidence supporting your negative assumptions and fears. For example, if you have decided to harm yourself because you felt you were unable to cope, consider the following questions as counter-evidence

How did you manage to:

- Arrive at your age?
- Parent children?
- Maintain employment?
- Maintain any relationship?
- Manage past stressors without hurting yourself?

Complete the following chart; examples are provided to assist you.

The Disputation Chart

Situation: *Too many bad things happened this week.*

Belief: *I have to harm myself to get relief.*

Proof Supporting Belief	Refuting Statement
1. *If I harm myself, I won't have to deal with anything.*	1. *I can try talking to my therapist and learn new ways to cope.*
2. *If I harm myself, my problems will go away.*	2. *I can try talking to my therapist and make a plan to tackle the problems.*
3. _____	3. _____
4. _____	4. _____
5. _____	5. _____
6. _____	6. _____

WORKSHEET 13
Behavioral Triggers

What specific behaviors did you engage in before, during, and after you wanted to harm yourself? Did you notice that you had felt withdrawn just before you became especially vulnerable to self-harm? Were you having an argument with a significant other?

Before:

Behavior 1 _____ .

Behavior 2 _____ .

Behavior 3 _____ .

During:

Behavior 1 _____ .

Behavior 2 _____ .

Behavior 3 _____ .

After:

Behavior 1 _____ .

Behavior 2 _____ .

Behavior 3 _____ .

Detail as much information regarding your behaviors as possible. Use the lines below.

_____

_____

_____

_____

_____

_____

_____

_____

_____

_____ .

WORKSHEET 14
Behavioral Triggers & Suggested Interventions

Scan the list you just made and identify which specific behaviors you wish to address.

Behavior 1 _____.

Behavior 2 _____.

Behavior 3 _____.

The following interventions can help you alter your behaviors related to self-harm.

Complete WORKSHEET 15: THE EXPANDED INCIDENT CHART. As self-harm can be distressing, overwhelming, and, at times, lethal, it is important to examine in detail all of the warning signs that indicate self-harm. Again, consider what you were experiencing prior to the act of self-harm or suicide. The goal is not only to learn to identify when self-harm is more likely, but also to note early alarms so that you can generate new and different options.

The EXPANDED INCIDENT CHART for self-harm includes a column marked *People*. This section is meant to help you identify if there are certain situations and events combined with particular individuals (in conjunction with situations and events) that tend to prompt thoughts of self-harm. Perhaps you have noticed that you are compelled to harm yourself when you are feeling distressed, hopeless, or defeated in relation to a particular individual in a particular event.

WORKSHEET 15
The Expanded Incident Chart

Think about the situation you described in WORKSHEET 2: THE ASSIGNMENT and ask yourself the following:

- What was I physically experiencing before, during, and after the situation?
- What was I feeling?
- What thoughts were running through my mind before, during, and after the situation?
- How was I behaving? [*name some specific behaviors*]
- Is there a specific person or group associated with this situation?

Now fill out the worksheet in as much detail as possible.

Situation: _____.

Prior to Incident

People	Physiological sensations	Emotions	Cognitions/ thoughts	Behaviors
_____.	_____.	_____.	_____.	_____.
_____.	_____.	_____.	_____.	_____.

During Incident

People	Physiological sensations	Emotions	Cognitions/ thoughts	Behaviors
_____.	_____.	_____.	_____.	_____.
_____.	_____.	_____.	_____.	_____.

After Incident

People	Physiological sensations	Emotions	Cognitions/ thoughts	Behaviors
_____.	_____.	_____.	_____.	_____.
_____.	_____.	_____.	_____.	_____.

Avoid the Situation

When things are getting difficult, I can go _____

_____.

Identify a Friend

This person can be like an anchor. You should identify someone who is soothing and does not trigger you.

When I am overwhelmed or feel hopeless I can call [*add names and phone numbers*]:

_____

_____

_____

_____.

Identify an Anchor

An anchor is similar to a friend, but it doesn't necessarily need to be a person. An anchor can be any thought that helps you to feel grounded or safe. For instance, you can remember a prior time when you felt really safe and grounded. Describe this experience.

_____

_____

_____.

Create a Safety Plan

Use this safety plan when you experience urges to become self-injurious. (Complete with your therapist.)

When I have an urge to self-harm, my safety plan is to:

_____

_____

_____

_____.

Consider Your Triggers

Address the factors that lead you to self-harm and be on guard for them. As you piece everything together, consider all of your physical, emotional, cognitive, behavioral, and situational triggers (including other people) that contribute to your warning signs that tend to lead to self-harm. Specifically, what situations tend to make you act in this way? Try to conjure up times when the feelings and emotions inside just seemed unbearable. Where were you? Was it after a fight or argument? Or maybe a long day's work? If you are able to write as many of these situations on WORKSHEET 15, you can begin to discern a pattern of what your own triggers are.

Reward Yourself

Do something good for yourself in exchange for not harming yourself (e.g., take time for a favorite book).

Consider the Consequences

Review the following negative outcomes of self-harm:

- Self-harm can be irreversible.
- Self-harm upsets and disturbs others close to yo.
- Self-harm causes scarring and permanent reminders.
- Self-harm may lead to an even worse situations (e.g., life support, brain damage, hurting someone else in the process).
- Self-harm is a short-term solution.
- Self-harm may lead to a family legacy of suicide.

Remember, you are unique and *not replaceable*!

Identify the Behavior Chain

The following BEHAVIORAL CHAIN or flow chart can be used to identify specific areas that you can intervene when self-harm is a possibility.

Behavior Chain*

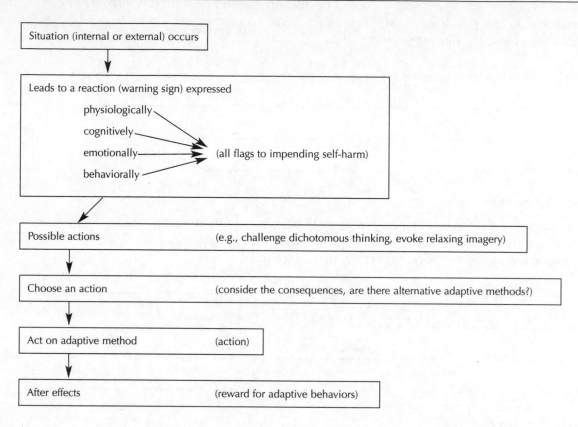

*(Adapted from J. Pretzer [1990]. Borderline personality disorder. In A. Beck, A. Freeman, & Associates [eds.], *Cognitive therapy of personality disorders* [pp. 176–207]. New York: Guilford Press. Reprinted by permission of the Guilford Press, 1990©.)

You can use this behavior chain as a means to help with decision-making and diverting the urge to self-harm. It allows for a more controlled method of reviewing available options. Life is full of challenges and we are confronted with many difficult situations. Having some assistance in the decision-making process will allow you to feel empowered and enable you to choose not to harm yourself but rather to care for yourself. The goal is simple: To keep yourself safe and protected, and to give yourself the opportunity to identify all your options so that you continue to live without the constant cloud of suicide or self-harm over your head.

WORKSHEET 16
Situational Triggers

There are times, individuals, events, and places that trigger you to self-harm. Knowing which situations cause you difficulty can help you be prepared if a similar situation occurs; in particular, you can be on alert for your alarms. You identified your four areas of warning signs in WORKSHEET 3: THE INCIDENT CHART. Now list the situations in which you tend to be especially vulnerable to harming yourself. You might be able to identify certain times of the week, people you are around, or different types of situations that tend to make you feel overwhelmed and helpless. Review WORKSHEET 1 if you need help identifying these situations.

1. _____

_____

_____.

2. _____

_____

_____.

3. _____

_____

_____.

4. _____

_____

_____.

5. _____

_____.

6. _____

_____

_____.

WORKSHEET 17
Situational Triggers & Suggested Interventions

WORKSHEET 16 identifies those situations in which you have harmed yourself. If you are in a situation similar to or included in that list, the following interventions can help you avoid self-harm.

Remove Yourself

If you find yourself in a situation where in the past you have harmed yourself, you can choose to remove yourself from that specific environment. For example, if you know that attending a memorial service or funeral causes intense pain and depression, you can decide whether attending the service is something you really need to do. Or, if you do attend, you can make sure you do so with the support of a friend and only spend a limited time offering your respects.

When things get particularly difficult, I can _____

_____

_____

_____

_____

_____.

Try Something Different

What can you do other than self-harm? Can you try other means of creating a sense of relief? Carry a list of these "other things to do." Here are some alternative behaviors (Layden, Newman, Freeman, & Morse, 1993, p. 62) that you can try when you experience thoughts or impulses to self-harm. (To ensure safety, please review with your therapist before attempting some of these exercises.)

- Telephone an on-call therapist or professional.
- Telephone a sympathetic friend or relative.
- Go to the emergency room of the nearest hospital.
- Hit oneself with pillows.
- Use a water-soluble, red felt-tip pen to write on oneself as an alternative to cutting with a sharp object.
- Immerse one's hand in cold water.
- Crunch raw eggs on oneself.
- Spend an hour reviewing an audiotape from a therapy session.
- Spend an hour reviewing old therapy homework assignments.
- Spend an hour applying various self-help skills.

Instead of _____ [*behavior*],

I can try _____

_____

_____

_____

_____.

The DPS

Your therapist will help you complete this worksheet.

Date of Assessment: _____

FREEMAN DIAGNOSTIC PROFILING SYSTEM

(© FREEMAN, 2003) REVISED EDITION

Session#: _____ Evaluator: _____

Patient Name: _____ Patient#: _____ Location: _____

Birthdate: _____ Age: _____ Race: _____ Gender: _____ Birthorder: _____ Marital/Children: _____

Employment: _____ Education: _____ Disability: _____ Medication: _____

Physician: _____ Referral Question: _____

Instructions: Record the diagnosis including the code number. Briefly identify the criteria for the selected diagnosis. Working with the patient either directly as as part of the data gathering of the clinical interview, SCALE the SEVERITY of EACH CRITERION for the patient at the PRESENT TIME. Indicate the level of severity on the grid.

DIAGNOSIS (DSM/ICD) with Code:

Axis I: _____

Axis II: _____

Axis III: _____

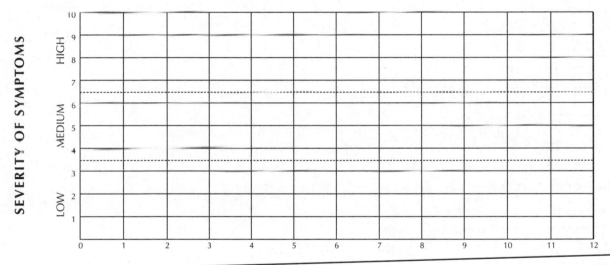

DESCRIPTIVE CRITERIA

CRITERIA:

1 _____   7 _____

2 _____   8 _____

3 _____   9 _____

4 _____   10 _____

5 _____   11 _____

6 _____   12 _____

Do you believe that the above noted criteria are a reaonably accurate sample of the patient's behavior? **YES** or **NO**

If **NO**, please indicate why: _____

Are there any reasons to believe that this individual is an imminent danger to himself/herself or others? **YES** or **NO**

If **YES**, please indicate the danger: _____

(From Freeman, 1998.)

CHALLENGING WHAT YOU KNOW & DO: TAKING CONTROL

The treatment goals related to self-harm or injury are to keep you safe. There are different ways to help with this, but it begins with you. (That includes the very fact that you have completed this section!) You are taking steps to take charge of protecting yourself. Although you may have felt very down and even hopeless, suicide is not the answer. Even though you may be someone who has a pattern of self-harm, you can tackle that pattern and disrupt the cycle. You can, by identifying particularly painful times and watching your alarm system, choose to stay safe and even become your own safe person.

| **CHAPTER 6** | Emotional Control: Too Many Moods in Too Little Time |

As humans, we are moody. We experience many emotions not only within a given day, but even within shorter lengths of time. We can rapidly shift from feeling great to feeling lousy, all without apparent conscious control and sometimes in just a matter of moments. In fact, it may take only a few seconds for your body to respond to a particular stimulus. We may not even have recognized that we have shifted moods until someone asks us, "What's wrong?" or "What's the matter?"

In addition to having fluctuating emotions, as someone who is sensitive to internal states and external surroundings, you might have noticed that you sometimes become alternatively tearful, anxious, or happy for a brief period of time. At times these emotional states can be extreme; you can even become volatile. If your internal states are perilously balanced and highly reactive to the external world, you might feel like you are on an emotional seesaw. This is because your mood depends primarily on things outside yourself and over which you have little or no control. Perhaps you experience constant ups and downs, never reaching an equilibrium point. Your own sensitivity could have allowed someone else's offhand or joking comment, sideways glance, or more direct slight to cause a radical change in your mood. You might have quickly shifted from a relatively good mood to a state of anger, frustration, irritability, tenseness, and sadness.

Have you been described as "moody"? Have you noticed that generally your mood shifts are in response to something or someone in particular? Your mood states are often a product not only of someone else's responses to you, but also of how you have perceived, filtered, and interpreted incoming information. Fluctuating mood states are also often a result of reacting to something that we think has occurred or are fearing will occur. Usually moodiness is something that doesn't feel good or right.

As you may well know, mood shifts and emotional reactivity are quite exhausting both for oneself and others. You might not be able to identify "quiet" times when you were not reacting, but rather, relaxing with yourself or others. If you become angry, perhaps you have said something that you later regretted and subsequently kicked yourself for not thinking of the consequences. When you were feeling down and vulnerable you might have opened up to someone you barely knew and later regretted sharing so much of yourself. Unfortunately, when mood shifts are a central part of your life, your friends might not believe you are dependable or reliable. They might not know who is joining them on any given day—the happy person or the person sobbing over dinner.

This chapter will help you learn to take control of your mood swings and achieve a better balance. Remember, everyone has ups and downs. But you might have noticed that your moods shift more often and more radically than those of others. You might also never feel that you're able to relax completely or be content with your current mood. The greater goal is to recognize the times when your mood shifts make you more likely to behave in ways that you will later regret, and to identify new ways to lift yourself up when you experience sadness.

VIGNETTES

Vignette 1: Jackie

Jackie was in a great mood. She knew that Bob would be calling her around 10:00 A.M. to make final plans for the evening. Everything was set. It made doing her work so much easier. She was plowing through the stack of typing her supervisor left for her on her desk. She giggled at her officemate's colorful calendar and thought that she even looked good today. When Bob hadn't called by 10:15, Jackie's mood took a terrible nosedive. "Why hasn't he called?" she thought. "He's dumping me; I just know it." Jackie's tears streamed down her face as she considered another failed relationship. She snapped at her supervisor, lost the material she was typing, and flew into the bathroom sobbing—ultimately missing Bob's call.

Vignette 2: Ellie

Ellie was on her way to work. She drove the same route, at the same time, every day. It was a nice, clear, crisp autumn morning. When she left her apartment complex she saw that there was some ice on her windshield. She also saw that a man was scraping the ice from her neighbor, Susan's, windshield. Ellie immediately felt down. "I don't have anyone to do that for me," she thought.

As she pulled out onto the street, a big, black Mercedes cut in front of her. Ellie was furious. "Who the hell does that bastard think he is!?" she thought. She began cursing at the driver and tried to chase him and flip him the bird. Eventually, she lost him in the traffic.

The drive to work had less traffic than usual. Ellie enjoyed the sunshine, and the oldies station was playing some of her favorite songs. "Gosh, I miss those songs," she thought. She started to feel weepy as she pulled into the parking lot at work. "Here it is only 8:45 in the morning, and I feel exhausted," she thought.

Review the Vignettes

Do either of these scenarios sound familiar to you? In both situations the characters experienced rapid changes in their mood due to internal and external events. In the first situation, Jackie's mood was shifted by an outside event (Bob's not calling on time), which led to a negative thought and assumption (he's dumping me), which, in turn, affected her emotional state. As a response to that negative thought, she behaved irresponsibly at work. Ellie's moods shifted repeatedly in reaction to the many things happening around her.

Because mood shifts are a product of not only outside events but also of how we perceive and interpret them, we can learn to take control of our moods. Again, this can occur if you not only learn to recognize when you are experiencing mood changes, but when also you try to identify the *cause* of the mood change. Once you are able to identify the cause of the mood change, you have information to contextualize, control, and challenge your immediate perception of what is happening. Our thoughts have powerful effects on how we feel. Would things have been different for Jackie if she knew that Bob was late calling her because he was stuck in a traffic jam? Would she then have interpreted differently his not calling exactly at 10:00? If she had interpreted things differently, she might not have experienced such a rapid change of mood and ultimately a radical change in behavior.

WHAT YOU WOULD LIKE TO CHANGE

First discuss with your therapist whether this seems to be area that is problematic for you. Do you relate to the vignettes? Does this behavior appear to occur in a pattern? Is it an area of your life over which you wish you had more control? If it does not seem pertinent, discuss with your therapist whether you need to continue to the assessment section.

SELF-MONITORING: HOW DO I KNOW WHAT MY PERCEPTIONS ARE?

Keep one theme in mind: control. You are not a pure product or victim of your emotions. Although your mood states can feel out of your control, you do have control over what you do with them. How we respond to mood changes has a great effect on whether they become better or worse. How many times have you noticed that just when you're starting to be in a bad mood, someone is cracking a joke that suddenly makes you smile and start to feel good again? The progression of your bad mood was stopped because you received good (in this case, funny) information. In essence, this is what we'd like to help you learn to do—to learn to recognize when your mood has changed and to step in and alter its course to a better or more comfortable state. This begins with your understanding how you perceive the environment and how that perception affects your mood states.

The way to understand how you perceive things is to self-monitor. The way we sense, interpret, and process information from the outside environment has a bearing on our own internal world; we react emotionally to this combination of information from the outside world and our own assumptions (schemas). How do you interpret what is being said to you? Do you usually put a negative "spin" on things? Do you usually interpret things through a dark filter? Do you tend to see things in black and white? These types of thinking patterns usually contribute to a negative mood state, but they can be challenged. However, the only way to challenge them is to start to monitor what they actually are.

THE WORKSHEETS

The following section includes several worksheets that address the current chapter topic. The worksheets are designed to help you learn more about yourself so that you can decide if there is anything you wish to change. Your therapist can help you use them.

WORKSHEET 1
The Assessment

Rate the severity of the following problems as you think they may relate to you.

0 = none   1 = mild   2 = moderate   3 = severe   4 = extremely severe

1. Friends/colleagues have described you as being moody.   ___

2. You experience many mood changes throughout the day.   ___

3. Your friends would describe you as intense.   ___

4. Your mood can fluctuate very rapidly and with little provocation.   ___

5. You find it difficult to think of a time when you are in a neutral mood.   ___

6. You have done impulsive things in response to your mood changes.   ___

7. You become irritated, frustrated, and angry very easily.   ___

8. You have disclosed private details about yourself to new acquaintances.   ___

9. When you become emotionally overwhelmed you cry, yell, or snap at someone.   ___

10. You wake up each day not knowing how you'll feel.   ___

If you answered several of the items as the usual way you experience moods, you might be experiencing rapid mood changes. At times you might feel exhausted from trying to keep up with yourself and all of your mood changes and long for a quiet, peaceful existence.

WORKSHEET 2
The Assignment

Think of the last time you experienced a huge mood shift in a short period of time. You felt the mood shift intensely. You might have experienced a mood change due to what someone said to you or to an experience you had. Others might even have said, "What happened?" or "Why are you suddenly down in the dumps?" Take a moment to remember a time like this. Use the lines below to detail your experience. Be as specific as possible. You will compile your reactions in WORKSHEET 3: THE INCIDENT CHART.

_____

_____

_____

_____

_____

_____

_____

_____

_____

_____

_____

_____

_____

_____

_____

_____

_____

_____

_____

_____

WORKSHEET 3
The Incident Chart*

This worksheet will help you begin uncovering the schema related to this characteristic. Think about the situation you described in WORKSHEET 2 and ask yourself the following:

- What was I physically experiencing before, during, and after the situation?
- What was I feeling?
- What thoughts were running through my mind before, during, and after the situation?
- How was I behaving? [*name some specific behaviors*]

Now fill out the worksheet in as much detail as possible.

Situation: _____

_____

Prior to Incident

Physiological sensations	Emotions	Cognitions/ thoughts	Behaviors
_____	_____	_____	_____
_____	_____	_____	_____
_____	_____	_____	_____
_____	_____	_____	_____

During Incident

Physiological sensations	Emotions	Cognitions/ thoughts	Behaviors
_____	_____	_____	_____
_____	_____	_____	_____
_____	_____	_____	_____
_____	_____	_____	_____

After Incident

Physiological sensations	Emotions	Cognitions/ thoughts	Behaviors
_____	_____	_____	_____
_____	_____	_____	_____
_____	_____	_____	_____
_____	_____	_____	_____

*(Adapted from J. S. Beck, *Cognitive Therapy: Basics and Beyond.* Guilford Press, 1995©.)

WORKSHEET 4
The DTR*

This worksheet is designed to assist you identifying your automatic thoughts. Noting your automatic thoughts can help you to determine what underlying schemas or beliefs are related to particular events or situations. What are your automatic thoughts relating to your mood shifts? Do you experience thoughts such as "I have no control over my moods"? Your therapist will help you with the rest.

Date/Time	Situation	Automatic thought	Emotion	Adaptive response	Outcome

*(Adapted from J. S. Beck, *Cognitive Therapy: Basics and Beyond.* Guilford Press, 1995©.)

WORKSHEET 5
Schemas

What are your rules or schemas related to your mood shifts? Take a moment to write them down.

_____

_____

_____

_____

_____

_____

_____

Choose any of the specific rules that and fill in each of the columns. Indicate what each rule is, where (or whom) it comes from, what meaning it has for you, and how likely or easy it would be for you to change that rule. Once you have identified your particular schemas, how strong they are, and whether or not they can be changed, you can begin to create treatment goals.

Schema	Where it comes from	Meaning to me	Easy to change?

WORKSHEET 6
Treatment Goals

This worksheet asks you to identify your treatment goals, the symptoms that prevent you from obtaining your goals, the schemas that are associated with those goals, and the change that you are hoping for. Are you able to imagine yourself completing the goals? Complete this chart with the help of your therapist and prioritize the importance of each of these goals.

	Symptoms that prevent you from obtaining goal	Schema associated with goal	Hoped-for change	Realistic or unrealistic?	How outcome looks if goal is reached
Goal 1: Highest priority					
Goal 2: High priority					
Goal 3: Moderate priority					
Goal 4: Low priority					

Your therapist will help you complete this worksheet.

Date of Assessment: _____

FREEMAN DIAGNOSTIC PROFILING SYSTEM

Session#: _____ Evaluator: _____

(© FREEMAN, 2003) REVISED EDITION

Patient Name: _____ Patient#: _____ Location: _____

Birthdate: _____ Age: _____ Race: _____ Gender: _____ Birthorder: _____ Marital/Children: _____

Employment: _____ Education: _____ Disability: _____ Medication: _____

Physician: _____ Referral Question: _____

Instructions: Record the diagnosis including the code number. Briefly identify the criteria for the selected diagnosis. Working with the patient either directly as as part of the data gathering of the clinical interview, SCALE the SEVERITY of EACH CRITERION for the patient at the PRESENT TIME. Indicate the level of severity on the grid.

DIAGNOSIS (DSM/ICD) with Code:

Axis I: _____

Axis II: _____

Axis III: _____

SEVERITY OF SYMPTOMS — HIGH / MEDIUM / LOW

DESCRIPTIVE CRITERIA

CRITERIA:

1 _____   7 _____

2 _____   8 _____

3 _____   9 _____

4 _____   10 _____

5 _____   11 _____

6 _____   12 _____

Do you believe that the above noted criteria are a reaonably accurate sample of the patient's behavior? **YES** or **NO**

If **NO**, please indicate why: _____

Are there any reasons to believe that this individual is an imminent danger to himself/herself or others? **YES** or **NO**

If **YES**, please indicate the danger: _____

(From Freeman, 1998.)

WORKSHEET 7
Physical Triggers

Physical sensations are clues to help you avoid future distressful situations. Think of the experience you described in WORKSHEET 2: THE ASSIGNMENT. What were you experiencing physically prior to, during, and after your mood change? Were you feeling wound up? You might have felt some of the following:

- queasy stomach.
- sweating/clammy skin.
- racing heart.
- tension.
- GI distress.

Use the lines below to describe your physical sensations.

_____

_____

_____

_____

_____

_____

_____

_____

_____

_____

_____

_____

_____

_____

_____

_____

_____

_____

WORKSHEET 8
Physical Triggers & Suggested Interventions

Three techniques can help you combat physiological distress: (1) take a moment to stop; (2) employ relaxation techniques; and (3) use relaxing imagery.

Stop

In WORKSHEET 4, you identified the thoughts that directly related to your mood shifts and changes. For this exercise, identify the thoughts that seem to be creating or exacerbating uncomfortable physical reactions. Use the lines below to write down those thoughts.

_____

_____

_____

_____

_____

_____ .

If you notice that you are experiencing the warning signs from your physical system that a mood change is likely to occur, take a moment to stop the process. For example, if you get an upset stomach when you feel down, stop.

You can do this by _____

_____

_____

_____

_____ .

Relax

In WORKSHEET 3, you identified what specific physical symptoms occur when you are having mood shifts or changes. If you know what physical symptoms are related to problems with your moods, use relaxation after you have taken a moment to stop. This can be as simple as just sitting down and taking a few deep breaths. Once you have stopped, take a moment to relax. Try some deep breathing and centering. I can relax by

_____

_____

_____

_____

_____ .

Relaxing Imagery

While you are relaxing, imagine your safe place. You may even want to put a "happy" spin on it; in other words, you are feeling really good in your safe place.

I feel safe imagining _____

_____

_____.

I hear _____

_____

_____.

I feel _____

_____

_____.

I can see _____

_____

_____.

I can smell _____

_____

_____.

I can taste _____

_____

_____.

My safe person who can join me here is _____

_____

_____.

WORKSHEET 9
Emotional Triggers

How would you describe the emotions you had around the time of your mood change? As your feelings are intricately connected to your overall mood state, it is important to understand which feelings appear to trigger an overall mood shift. Perhaps you have experienced difficulty even identifying the actual mood state that you are experiencing. Part of self-monitoring involves understanding and recognizing when or if a mood change has occurred. You will utilize this information for the interventions. Use WORKSHEETS 3 and 4 to identify some of the feelings you had when you experienced a mood change. They might include some of the following:

- fear.
- anger.
- sadness.
- disgust.

What were you feeling emotionally? Write down what those feelings were like.

_____

_____

_____

_____

_____

_____

_____

_____

_____

_____

_____

_____

_____

_____

_____

_____

WORKSHEET 10
Emotional Triggers & Suggested Interventions

Part of self-monitoring involves understanding and recognizing when or if a mood change has occurred. Learning exactly what these mood states feel like and are associated with will help you predict mood-state changes and give you the opportunity to control them.

Identify Mood States

Let's begin by looking at some basic mood states and how you can learn to identify whether you're experiencing one of them. Jackie, in the first vignette, is used as an example to demonstrate how warning flags precipitate mood changes. Fill in how you identify your mood states. (Examples are provided to assist you.)

My happy mood states are related to:

Thoughts including   *He likes me, I'm okay.*

Behaviors including *Giddiness, laughing, working hard.*

Bodily sensations including   *Butterflies in stomach.*

Feelings including *Excitement, anticipation.*

My bad mood states are related to:

Thoughts including *Being ignored/dumped.*

Behaviors including *Losing concentration, snapping.*

Bodily sensations including *Tightness in the chest.*

Feelings including *Despair, hopelessness.*

If Jackie had self-monitored she would have been able to identify how her mood changed when she perceived that Bob had dumped her. She then would have had the opportunity to jump in and change how she was feeling. Once you begin monitoring for any of the previous signs, you can make decisions about how you want to handle your mood.

Scale Back

Pick one of the uncomfortable emotional responses you wish to address from WORKSHEET 9. On a scale of 1 to 10 (1 being least severe and 10 being most severe), rate the severity of the emotion you experienced during the mood shift.

    1   2   3   4   5   6   7   8   9   10

As you continue to have uncomfortable emotions related to mood shifts, scale back or "turn the oven down." You might want to combine scaling back with some relaxation techniques described in WORKSHEET 8 on physical triggers. Once you have turned yourself down, rate your emotions again.

    1   2   3   4   5   6   7   8   9   10

How did you do? Were you able to turn yourself down? You'll notice that with practice, turning down your own emotional temperature becomes easier and easier. Can you describe how you are feeling now?

_____

_____

_____

_____

_____

_____

_____

_____

_____

_____

_____

WORKSHEET 11
Cognitive/Automatic Thoughts

What thoughts were running through your mind before, during, and after your mood change? Do any particular types of thoughts seem to change how you are feeling? Often these thoughts can exacerbate or exaggerate a mood. Do you experience thoughts such as "If things don't go right, my mood seems to change"? Refer to WORKSHEET 4: THE DTR to help identify the specific thoughts related to this topic. Write your responses below.

WORKSHEET 12
Cognitive/Automatic Thoughts & Suggested Interventions

Thoughts often affect your mood. The following techniques can help you examine the thoughts that change your mood and to learn to challenge those thoughts that cause upsetting or distressful moods.

Challenge Catastrophic Thinking

Jackie's catastrophic interpretation of the situation led to a rapid and negative mood change. Do you tend to assume the worst? What catastrophic thoughts tend to make you upset or cause a change in your mood? For example, if someone cuts you off while driving, do you automatically think, "Everyone is awful!" which leads to changes in your mood? Can you challenge the thought with "Some people are inconsiderate, but not *all* people."

The Catastrophic Thinking Chart		
Situation	Catastrophic thought	Noncatastrophic thought
_____ .	_____ .	_____ .
_____	_____	_____
_____	_____	_____
_____	_____	_____
_____	_____	_____
_____	_____	_____
_____	_____	_____
_____	_____	_____

Although negative events do occur in life, is it *every* time? Challenge your own catastrophic thoughts with outcomes that oppose them. Although our worst fears may become real, is this always the case? Are there times when your catastrophic assumptions have been wrong? Try to create that middle ground where there very well could be another explanation for events not going as you want them. Considering this middle ground can directly affect how you are feeling and may help prevent your mood swings.

Challenge Black-and-White Thinking

Utilize the artist's pallette of black and white and mix them to form the grays of life. What else might have prevented Jackie's boyfriend from calling? What's the in-between? Thinking in grays can give you a much more positive (and less frightening!) view of many situations, as well as the ability to consider more than just one scenario. What are your catastrophic thoughts related to? Can you name some of the grays? (An example is provided to assist you.)

The Dichotomous Thinking Chart

Black	Gray(s)	White
	--	--	
He's leaving me.	He didn't call because he's stuck in traffic. I can relax and seek support.	He's perfect.

_____. _____. _____

_____. _____. _____

_____. _____. _____

_____. _____. _____

I have a hard time mixing grays related to _____

_____

_____

_____.

Weigh the Evidence

Look at the negative assumptions you tend to make when you experience a mood shift or change. Challenge yourself to prove those assumptions, and provide a refuting statement. (Examples are provided to assist you.)

The Disputation Chart

Situation. Friend forgot your birthday.

Belief: Friends let me down.

Proof Supporting Belief	Refuting Statement
1. Friend did not call or send card.	1. Many people make honest mistakes.
2. Friends can be disappointing.	2. Many friends have come through for me.
3. _____.	3. _____.
4. _____.	4. _____.
5. _____.	5. _____.
6. _____.	6. _____.

Handling Emotions

If you experience a change in mood or are feeling out of control, take moment to remind yourself that:

You can handle yourself in times of crisis.

You have handled _____.

You are handling _____.

You have many good qualities that will not go away just because you're moody.

You are an individual who has many options in life.

WORKSHEET 13
Behavioral Triggers

What specific behaviors did you engage in before, during, and after you experienced a mood change? Were you alone? Were you listening to something or trying to relax? Were you doing an activity that reminded you of something or someone?

Before:

Behavior 1 _____.

Behavior 2 _____.

Behavior 3 _____.

During:

Behavior 1 _____.

Behavior 2 _____.

Behavior 3 _____.

After:

Behavior 1 _____.

Behavior 2 _____.

Behavior 3 _____.

Detail as much information regarding your behaviors as possible. Use the lines below.

_____

_____

_____

_____

_____

_____

_____

_____

_____

_____.

WORKSHEET 14
Behavioral Triggers & Suggested Interventions

Scan the list you just made and identify which behaviors you wish to address.

Behavior 1 _____.

Behavior 2 _____.

Behavior 3 _____.

The following interventions can help you alter your behaviors in response to experiencing a mood shift.

Consider Triggers

Consider triggers in depth. Review WORKSHEET 3 and be sure that you have identified the things that seem to bring about a mood change.

Validate Self and Emotions

Remind yourself that you can handle yourself in emotional situations.

Stop

Take a moment to stop before you act. In this way you can take time to consider the consequences.

Use Your Emotional Energy Better

Emotions can be draining. Have you ever noticed how tired you are after an emotional movie or event? Much energy gets used in creating, maintaining, and expressing rapid emotional shifts; try to funnel that energy toward something that benefits you. For instance, you could use your "anger" energy to complete a long-term project.

When I experience mood changes and shifts, I can direct my energy toward _____

_____

_____

_____

_____

_____

_____

_____

_____

_____.

Have a Backup Plan

Identify a backup plan for when you become moody. What can you do? Take a walk? Relax? Tackle a project?

When I become moody, I can _____

_____

_____

_____

_____

_____.

Identify a Friend

Call your safe person when you feel overwhelmed by your emotions.

When I am overwhelmed I can call/contact _____

_____

_____

_____.

Change Your Focus

Think of other things. Distract yourself. Put on a silly talkshow. Watch a movie you've wanted to see. Or read a magazine you've been dying to pore through.

WORKSHEET 16
Situational Triggers

There may be times, individuals, events, and places that seem to trigger your mood shifts. Knowing which situations cause you difficulty can help you be prepared if a similar situation occurs; in particular, you can be on alert for your alarms. You have identified your four areas of warning signs in WORKSHEET 3: THE INCIDENT CHART. Now list the situations in which you tend to be especially moody. Is it related to any particular part of your life? To particular people? You might be able to identify certain times of the week, people you are around, or different types of situations that tend to make you feel frustrated or anxious. Review WORKSHEET 1 if you need help identifying these situations.

1. _____

_____

_____.

2. _____

_____

_____.

3. _____

_____

_____.

4. _____

_____

_____.

5. _____

_____

_____.

6. _____

_____

_____.

WORKSHEET 17
Situational Triggers & Suggested Interventions

WORKSHEET 16 identifies those situations in which you have experienced mood shifts or changes. If you are in a situation similar to one included in that list, the following interventions can help you avoid or manage mood shifts and changes.

Remove Yourself

For those situations that you have identified as triggering intense mood changes, remember that you can always remove yourself from this type of situation. Once you have recognized your internal alarms indicating an unpleasant mood change, take control and attempt to alter the situation by removing yourself. For instance, if you are at a party and begin to recognize a mood change related to your belief that no one at the party will want talk with you, you can choose to leave and call a friend.

When things get particularly difficult, I can _____

_____

_____

_____

_____

_____

_____

_____.

Try Something Different

If you are in an identified situation in which you know you are likely to experience a mood change, try something different from what you might normally do. For example, if you are in a social situation and are becoming upset due to negative thoughts about how attractive you are, challenge yourself to talk to at least two people concentrating only on the discussion, not physical appearance.

Instead of _____ [*behavior*],

I can try _____

_____

_____

_____

_____

_____

_____.

Your therapist will help you complete this worksheet.

Date of Assessment: _____

FREEMAN DIAGNOSTIC PROFILING SYSTEM

(© FREEMAN, 2003) REVISED EDITION

Session#: _____ Evaluator: _____

Patient Name: _____ Patient#: _____ Location: _____

Birthdate: _____ Age: _____ Race: _____ Gender: _____ Birthorder: _____ Marital/Children: _____

Employment: _____ Education: _____ Disability: _____ Medication: _____

Physician: _____ Referral Question: _____

Instructions: Record the diagnosis including the code number. Briefly identify the criteria for the selected diagnosis. Working with the patient either directly as as part of the data gathering of the clinical interview, SCALE the SEVERITY of EACH CRITERION for the patient at the PRESENT TIME. Indicate the level of severity on the grid.

DIAGNOSIS (DSM/ICD) with Code:

Axis I: _____

Axis II: _____

Axis III: _____

SEVERITY OF SYMPTOMS — HIGH / MEDIUM / LOW (vertical axis 1–10)

DESCRIPTIVE CRITERIA (horizontal axis 0–12)

CRITERIA:

1 _____   7 _____

2 _____   8 _____

3 _____   9 _____

4 _____   10 _____

5 _____   11 _____

6 _____   12 _____

Do you believe that the above noted criteria are a reaonably accurate sample of the patient's behavior? **YES** or **NO**

If **NO**, please indicate why: _____

Are there any reasons to believe that this individual is an imminent danger to himself/herself or others? **YES** or **NO**

If **YES**, please indicate the danger: _____

(From Freeman, 1998.)

CHALLENGING WHAT YOU KNOW & DO: TAKING CONTROL

Moods often are a result of volatile thoughts that add fuel to a burning fire. If you have identified yourself as a moody person or someone who experiences significant mood shifts, you probably feel as if you are sometimes held hostage by those feelings.

You might be unsure about how you will feel the next day; you might even begin to dread the new day. By not only watching for triggers and warning signs but also actually predicting and changing or preventing your mood shifts, you can begin to learn how to manage your moods. In other words, you can learn to take control.

CHAPTER 7

Feeling Empty: There Should Be Something Inside

There are times when we may have a "hollow" feeling inside, or be in a crowded room but still feel absolutely no connection with others. Although we know it shouldn't be that way, it is the way we feel. We may feel that our lives are empty, vacant, or bereft of any meaning or emotion. Sometimes it is a constant, gnawing feeling. Sometimes it is more episodic. In either case, it is very painful.

How does a feeling of emptiness start? Perhaps as children we learned that life was painful and intolerable. We might have learned that feelings were difficult and were to be avoided. The meaning of life was merely to survive from day to day. Life may have had meaning only because of the external structures of school, church, or home. Many children respond to this by retreating into an inner world of fantasy or by juggling emotions in an attempt to feel *something* and to give life *some* meaning. If we learned that if we had feelings, we were vulnerable to getting hurt, rejected, or humiliated, we might have decided it wasn't safe to feel anything at all. These patterns could have created a method for us to cope with everyday stressors and challenges. This approach, however, has the devastating consequence of leading to feelings of emptiness.

Sometimes you may vacillate between being feeling empty and being hypersensitive. Can they coexist? Yes, they can. When you finally feel, you may be so exquisitely aware of the emotions that you react to stimulation more than would others. You might be incredibly sensitive to changes in your emotional state. If you feel you are without feelings, identifying not only who you are but also your life's purpose becomes an overwhelming proposition. Some excitement interspersed with lengthy periods of sheer boredom can make you feel that you exist without a consistent plan or drive in life. Perhaps you do not feel connected to or part of things or others. Without any direction or feelings to guide you (remember the ship in the sea?), you may end up seeking relief (feeling for the sake of feeling) in stimulating and at times self-destructive activities. The consequences of these actions only become apparent when those things that were stimulating are no longer available, and you are again left with your internal vacancy.

In truth, however, you really are not empty at all. You just need to *turn up* your sensations a bit.

VIGNETTES

Vignette 1: Pam

It seemed like it would never end. The tight sensation in her chest proved that she was different.

Being different seemed as much a part of her as did her arms and legs. There was nothing to look forward to or be excited about, no one to help fill the void inside her. The boredom she felt was turning into despair. She thought of her colleagues at work, always smiling, humming, looking forward to the long weekend ahead. "Why are they able to feel and I can't?" thought Pam. She then decided to respond to the flirtations of the man sitting across the bar. "If I don't have feelings," thought Pam, "I'll just make them." She strained to see the tattoos covering his muscular arms and decided to ignore his wedding ring. She had to—she was finally experiencing a spark of excitement inside, a feeling.

Vignette 2: Tom

"Here we go again," Tom thought. "I'm being excluded." When the topic of conversation shifted to something about which he had little interest, Tom felt an even greater separation from the group. His stomach knotted and he felt like he would never be able to eat in the cafeteria again. As he thought some more, he began to feel more like an outcast—not just excluded, but rejected. "I knew this would happen. Once people get to know me, they find out how boring and stupid I am," Tom thought. "I'm almost 26 years old and I feel like I have no personality at all." Tom began to focus on how much the other people in the group had going for them. Compared to them, he felt like an empty shell. Where did they get all of their ideas or their thoughts on all of these topics? As the hollow feeling in his chest grew, Tom sneaked away from the group too embarrassed to say good-bye.

Review the Vignettes

Are either of these stories familiar to you? In both scenarios, the characters experienced a pervasive sense of emptiness. We all sometimes lack direction, but for these characters it is an everyday experience that is extremely painful. They feel disconnected, hollow, and numb. Both react to their feelings of numbness or emptiness in a manner they later regret.

Note the warning signs that indicate emptiness. Pam had a sensation in her chest, was bored, and felt despair. Tom felt his stomach knot up, became anxious, and thought that he was stupid. Both characters then acted on these feelings with behavior that directly contradicted what they really wanted—an ongoing connection.

WHAT YOU WOULD LIKE TO CHANGE

First, discuss with your therapist whether this seems to be an area that is problematic for you. Do you relate to the vignettes? Does this behavior appear to occur as a pattern? Is it an area of your life over which you wish you had control? If it does not seem pertinent, discuss with your therapist whether you need to continue to the assessment section.

SELF-MONITORING: HOW DO I KNOW WHAT MY PERCEPTIONS ARE?

Can you make your life have meaning? One question to start with is whether you may be demanding so much from yourself, from others, and from life that it will be hard to get all you want. If you are unwilling to compromise, there is a problem. The fulfillment of most desires require you to make some compromises. Often people who seek to feel and experience everything in a powerful and intense way end up overlooking or ignoring the feelings that they *do* have. Or they experience feelings but have their sensor system turned down so low that they cannot interpret those feelings. If this is the case with you, you simply need to learn how to activate your alarm system.

How can you turn up your sensations and alarm system? Usually the goal is to turn them down. But, as mentioned in Chapter 1, you can experience emotions and experiences without necessarily interpreting them as such. This leads you to believe you are empty. Perhaps as a child you learned that life was empty, had no meaning; you just moved from crisis to crisis. Or perhaps you came to understand that life consisted only of pain, discomfort, or abuse; in order to deal with these difficulties, it was important for you not to feel.

However, as an adult, you have more options. You can protect and assert yourself, and also manage with those uncomfortable or painful situations. You no longer need the protective armor of emptiness that you put on when you decided, "It's safer not to feel."

How can you help yourself gain or regain meaning? The first step is to recognize that your feelings help give meaning to your life. Your feelings provide the clues or indicators of what is meaningful. Your empty feelings can make you feel as if you have no meaning or future direction. Similarly, out-of-control emotions may make you feel as if life has no direction or meaning. Simply put, our internal feeling world offers a structure for meaning. The external world helps to fill in that structure.

To help conceptualize this, picture a building under construction. First the workers build a shell or concrete framework that defines the structure (feelings). Then they add the roof, floors, and walls (meaning of life). We all must build the skeleton structure upon which the walls and floors of meaning will be set. The meaning of life, then, is something that we must organize internally. Feeling as if you are without this internal structure can be devastating. You are certainly not alone in this. Numerous people have struggled to define and identify their feelings. Philosophers have forever been trying to answer the questions "How do I feel?" and "What is the meaning of life?" So you are in very, very good company.

The goal of our program is to challenge the notion that there is no meaning in your life. You do have feelings; therefore, you have meaning. You probably just need a little help seeing that meaning. How can you learn to recognize that there is meaning in your life? Again, you must learn to read your system of sensors. They work well if you can read what they are saying. This will take practice; at times it can be frustrating, but you, too, can learn that you have meanings that are just waiting to be discovered. They might not be all that you want at first, but like a building under construction, you can build additions along the way.

THE WORKSHEETS

The following section includes several worksheets that address the current chapter topic. The worksheets are designed to help you learn more about yourself so that you can decide if there is anything you wish to change. Your therapist can help you use them.

WORKSHEET 1
The Assessment

Rate the severity of the following problems as you think they may relate to you.

0 = none   1 = mild   2 = moderate   3 = severe   4 = extremely severe

1. I feel lonely even in a group of people I know. ____

2. I often have the sensation of feeling emotionally hollow or empty inside. ____

3. People close to me often don't seem to satisfy my needs. ____

4. I often experience intolerable boredom. ____

5. I have been told by significant others that I am too needy or demanding. ____

6. My life seems to lack a sense of meaning or purpose. ____

7. I seek relief from boredom in potentially dangerous or self-destructive activities or outlets. ____

8. I often feel disconnected from the group I'm in; not really a part of things. ____

9. I struggle to feel connected or a part of anything. ____

10. I often feel as if I have no direction in life. ____

Does anything in the list seem familiar to you? Feeling disconnected and without a center can lead to extreme frustration and sadness. You might almost feel like a character from the *Wizard of Oz*—looking for a heart, a brain, and/or courage. You might believe that you were born without a component that everyone else has—a meaning to life or a sense of purpose.

WORKSHEET 2
The Assignment

Think of the last time you experienced feelings of emptiness. You might have felt all alone with no sense of meaning or direction and found it very distressing. Having others around you might not have changed the way you felt. Use the lines below to detail your experience. Be as specific as you can. You will compile your reactions in WORKSHEET 3: THE INCIDENT CHART.

_____

_____

_____

_____

_____

_____

_____

_____

_____

_____

_____

_____

_____

_____

_____

_____

_____

_____

_____

_____.

WORKSHEET 3
The Incident Chart*

This worksheet will help you begin uncovering the schemas related to this characteristic. Think about the situation you described in WORKSHEET 2 and ask yourself the following:

- What was I physically experiencing before, during, and after the situation?
- What was I feeling?
- What thoughts were running through my mind before, during, and after the situation?
- How was I behaving? [*name some specific behaviors*]

Now fill out the worksheet in as much detail as possible.

Situation: _____

_____.

Prior to Incident

Physiological sensations	Emotions	Cognitions/ thoughts	Behaviors
_____ .	_____ .	_____ .	_____ .
_____ .	_____ .	_____ .	_____ .
_____ .	_____ .	_____ .	_____ .
_____ .	_____ .	_____ .	_____ .

During Incident

Physiological sensations	Emotions	Cognitions/ thoughts	Behaviors
_____ .	_____ .	_____ .	_____ .
_____ .	_____ .	_____ .	_____ .
_____ .	_____ .	_____ .	_____ .
_____ .	_____ .	_____ .	_____ .

After Incident

Physiological sensations	Emotions	Cognitions/ thoughts	Behaviors
_____ .	_____ .	_____ .	_____ .
_____ .	_____ .	_____ .	_____ .
_____ .	_____ .	_____ .	_____ .
_____ .	_____ .	_____ .	_____ .

*(Adapted from J. S. Beck, *Cognitive Therapy: Basics and Beyond.* Guilford Press, 1995©.)

WORKSHEET 4
The DTR*

This worksheet is designed to assist you in identifying your automatic thoughts. Noting your automatic thoughts can help you determine what underlying schemas or beliefs relate to particular events or situations. What are your automatic thoughts related to emptiness? For example, do you experience thoughts such as "If I can't contribute to this conversation, I really don't have anything inside" or "When I'm not sure what to do, I know I have nothing inside"? Your therapist will help you with the rest.

Date/Time	Situation	Automatic thought	Emotion	Adaptive response	Outcome

*(Adapted from J. S. Beck, *Cognitive Therapy: Basics and Beyond.* Guilford Press, 1995©.)

WORKSHEET 5
Schemas

What are your rules or schemas related to feelings of emptiness? Take a moment to write them down.

_____

_____

_____

_____

_____

_____

_____.

Choose any of the specific rules and fill in each of the columns. Indicate what the rule is, where (or whom) it comes from, what meaning it has for you, and how likely or easy it would be for you to change that rule. Once you have identified your particular schemas, how strong they are, and whether or not they can be changed, you can begin to create treatment goals.

Schema	Where it comes from	Meaning to me	Easy to change?

WORKSHEET 6
Treatment Goals

This worksheet asks you to identify your treatment goals, the symptoms that prevent you from obtaining your goals, the schemas that are associated with those goals, and the change that you are hoping for. Are you able to imagine yourself completing the goals? Complete this chart with the help of your therapist and prioritize the importance of each of these goals.

	Symptoms that prevent you from obtaining goal	Schema associated with goal	Hoped-for change	Realistic or unrealistic?	How outcome looks if goal is reached
Goal 1: **Highest priority**					
Goal 2: **High priority**					
Goal 3: Moderate priority					
Goal 4: Low priority					

The DPS

Your therapist will help you complete this worksheet.

Date of Assessment: _____

FREEMAN DIAGNOSTIC PROFILING SYSTEM

(© FREEMAN, 2003) REVISED EDITION

Session#: _____ Evaluator: _____

Patient Name: _____ Patient#: _____ Location: _____

Birthdate: _____ Age: _____ Race: _____ Gender: _____ Birthorder: _____ Marital/Children: _____

Employment: _____ Education: _____ Disability: _____ Medication: _____

Physician: _____ Referral Question: _____

Instructions: Record the diagnosis including the code number. Briefly identify the criteria for the selected diagnosis. Working with the patient either directly as as part of the data gathering of the clinical interview, SCALE the SEVERITY of EACH CRITERION for the patient at the PRESENT TIME. Indicate the level of severity on the grid.

DIAGNOSIS (DSM/ICD) with Code:

Axis I: _____

Axis II: _____

Axis III: _____

CRITERIA:

1 _____   7 _____

2 _____   8 _____

3 _____   9 _____

4 _____   10 _____

5 _____   11 _____

6 _____   12 _____

Do you believe that the above noted criteria are a reaonably accurate sample of the patient's behavior? **YES** or **NO**

If **NO**, please indicate why: _____

Are there any reasons to believe that this individual is an imminent danger to himself/herself or others? **YES** or **NO**

If **YES**, please indicate the danger: _____

(From Freeman, 1998.)

WORKSHEET 7
A Physical Triggers

Physical sensations are clues to help you avoid future distressful situations. Think of the experience you described in WORKSHEET 2: THE ASSIGNMENT. What were you experiencing physically prior to, during, and after feeling alone, empty, and without meaning? It can be very difficult to describe these times, as the warning signs and alarms might not be as obvious as a feeling such as anger. You might have felt some of the following:

- queasy stomach.
- sweating/clammy skin.
- racing heart.
- tension.
- GI distress.

Use the lines below to describe your physical sensations.

_____

_____

_____

_____

_____

_____

_____

_____

_____

_____

_____

_____

_____

_____

_____

_____

WORKSHEET 8
Physical Triggers & Suggested Interventions

Three techniques can help you combat physiological distress: (1) take a moment to stop; (2) employ relaxation techniques; and (3) use relaxing imagery.

Stop

In Worksheet 4, you identified the thoughts directly related to your experience of feeling empty. For this exercise, identify the thoughts that seem to be creating or exacerbating uncomfortable physical reactions. Use the lines below to write down those thoughts.

_____

_____

_____

_____

_____

When you experience the physical component to feeling empty, such as a sinking feeling in your stomach or sweatiness, take a moment to stop. You need to give yourself the chance to look more closely at your feelingsand determine what is really going on. You can do this by

_____

_____

_____

_____

Relax

Try relaxation techniques such as deep breathing or even stretching. Feel how your body responds to your requests to relax. Reminding yourself of your physical body can help you remember that you are individual with a body, feelings, thoughts, and meaning.

When I am able to relax I notice my muscles _____

_____

When I am able to relax I notice my body _____

_____

When I am able to relax I notice my breathing _____

_____

When I am able to relax I notice my heartrate _____

_____

I have trouble relaxing when _____

_____ .

Now that you are aware of how your body relaxes or becomes tense, you can use this information to inform yourself when to use relaxation techniques and exercises.

Relaxing Imagery

Utilize your safe place as a special place that reinforces that you are an individual with unique likes, dislikes, and emotions.

I feel safe imagining _____

_____

_____ .

I hear _____

_____

_____ .

I feel _____

_____

_____ .

I can see _____

_____

_____ .

I can smell _____

_____

_____ .

I can taste _____

_____

_____ .

My safe person who can join me here is _____

_____

_____ .

WORKSHEET 9
Emotional Triggers

How would you describe the emotions you had before you experienced emptiness? They are particularly important, as they help define what types of feelings are uncomfortable for you and cause you to feel empty. Were you feeling lonely or sad? Were you angry? Use WORKSHEETS 3 and 4 to identify some of the feelings you had before you experienced emptiness. They might include some of the following:

- fear.
- anger.
- sadness.
- disgust.

What were you feeling emotionally? Write down what those feelings were like.

_____

_____

_____

_____

_____

_____

_____

_____

_____

_____

_____

_____

_____

_____

_____

_____

_____

_____

WORKSHEET 10
Emotional Triggers & Suggested Interventions

Emotions related to experiencing emptiness can be painful. Often people experience emptiness due to not knowing how they are feeling or "should" be feeling. You might notice that you don't feel things the same way others do and you might wonder why this is so. You do feel emotions; you just need to *turn them up* sometimes so you can tell what they are. We often associate our emotions with the meaning of our experience. If we are happy, we experience a feeling that says our meaning is good and that we understand what we want for ourselves. If we are unhappy, we question our meaning and try to figure out how to change it. It is therefore important for everyone to experience emotions in order to experience meaning.

The following interventions will help you with your emotions.

Exercise 1

This exercise asks you to complete the EXPERIENCES AND EMOTIONS CHART. This chart will help you identify daily experiences and their associated emotions. Go through a full day's worth of experiences and jot below those experiences that stood out. As our bodies, minds, behaviors, and emotions all interact, we need to be able to tease the pieces apart. All of the clues are there for you. What emotion do you attach to each experience? What did you experience physically? Remember that physical sensations and emotions are bidirectional. In other words, you can experience the physical sensation first and then have a feeling, or you can experience an emotion that prompts a bodily reaction. For example, if you notice your heart beating fast, what do you usually assume is happening? Are you afraid, excited, or happy? Now look at the emotions first: Have you ever noticed that when you are afraid your heart beats fast? Physiological sensations and emotional states combine to provide meaning for all of our experiences. Act as your own detective and investigate your experiences in detail. You can do this by turning up the power of your experience. You will probably be relieved that you, too, experience emotions and are not just an empty shell, but a fully-functioning member of the human race.

After you have completed the chart, review WORKSHEET 9: EMOTIONAL TRIGGERS; knowing that if a similar experience occurs, you can predict your emotion which will help you in future situations. You also know that the emotion exists, and you are not empty.

Pick a particular experience in the day and rank (from 1 to 5) your emotional state so as to predict what emotion will occur. (For example, if you had an argument with your boss and you notice that you are very angry and talking to him with a raised voice, what do you think the likelihood that if another disagreement occurs with your boss you would become angry?) How strongly you predict you would feel in the same situation provides you with important information about your emotions. Knowing that there is a strong likelihood that you would become angry again in a similar situation gives you an opportunity to better manage your anger (e.g., not raising your voice) and risking negative consequences.

The Experiences and Emotions Chart					
Rank the intensity of the felt emotion (e.g., anger, sadness, frustration) on a scale of 1 to 5, with 1 being the lowest intensity and 5 being the highest intensity. Because emotions are highly subjective, work with your therapist to establish the precise meaning of the ratings on this 5-point scale.					
Experience 1 _____.					
Physical sensation	**Thoughts**	**Behavior**	**Time of day**	**Emotion**	**Intensity**
				anger	
_____	_____	_____	_____	_____	_____.
_____	_____	_____	_____	_____	_____.
_____	_____	_____	_____	_____	_____.
_____	_____	_____	_____	_____	_____.
_____	_____	_____	_____	_____	_____.

Experience 2 _____.

Physical sensation	Thoughts	Behavior	Time of day	Emotion	Intensity
_____	_____	_____	_____	*anger* ___	___ .
_____	_____	_____	_____	_____	___ .
_____	_____	_____	_____	_____	___ .
_____	_____	_____	_____	_____	___ .
_____	_____	_____	_____	_____	___ .
_____	_____	_____	_____	_____	___ .

Exercise 2

By specifically looking at your experiences and emotions, you can begin to figure out what carries deep meaning in your life. The term *meaning* suggests an experience with associated feelings. In other words, feelings = meaning, and meaning = feelings. For example, if you experience a derogatory remark from a fellow staff member, the meaning becomes that actual experience. Attached to that experience is the thought "I'm no good at this job" or "I've failed again." Thus, the derogatory remark leads to "I'm no good" (meaning) = sadness (feeling).

How do your body, mind, and behaviors express emotions and meaning? By self-monitoring, you can learn to recognize the physiological sensations attached to the emotion, and by identifying the various emotional states you experience throughout the day directly contradicts the belief that you are empty. As you begin to define your experiences and the related emotions, the meanings of specific situations can now be identified. The MEANINGS CHART prompts you to connect your experiences to your emotions and derive meanings from them. The chart asks you to provide a summary of experiences or situations that provide meaning in your life (from Exercise 1). Next, you should list the attached emotion. From that emotion, identify the meaning of the experience. In order to help in this process, we have provided a list of words that may help you describe the meaning derived from the emotions you have in response to your experiences.

The following brief list of words can help you describe and define the meanings derived from your emotions:

loss	anger	happiness	specialness
acceptance	understanding	aggressiveness	tough-mindedness
fear	conscientiousness	sense of belonging	indifference
being overwhelmed	sensitivity	empowerment	

Now fill out the MEANINGS CHART; examples are provided to assist you.

The Meanings Chart

Experience	Emotion	=	Meaning
demand from boss	frustration		want to work independently
cut off in traffic	anger		don't like to be disregarded
_____ .	_____ .		_____
_____ .	_____ .		_____

What are some other ways to describe the meanings of your experiences? _____

_____

_____.

WORKSHEET 11
Cognitive/Automatic Thoughts

What thoughts were running through your mind before, during, and after you experienced emptiness? Were your thoughts related to any particular themes of being alone? being misunderstood? Perhaps you were thinking that you wished you felt more.

Refer to WORKSHEET 4: THE DTR to help identify the specific thoughts related to this topic. Write your responses below.

_____

_____

_____

_____

_____

_____

_____

_____

_____

_____

_____

_____

_____

_____

_____

_____

_____

_____

_____

_____

WORKSHEET 12
Cognitive/Automatic Thoughts & Suggested Interventions

Emptiness is often associated with particular feeling states. Some type of physiological arousal has been interpreted as an empty feeling. For example, if you feel a hollow pit in your stomach, you may think, "Oh no, here's that feeling of emptiness again" or "I'm all alone again and sad." Once that feeling state has been designated as emptiness, you might then experience despair and loneliness, and ultimately react in response to those feelings.

Try the following interventions.

Challenge Catastrophic Thinking

Do you tend to assume the worst? For example, if you are in a group of strangers with whom you have little in common, do you think, "I am nothing and alone?" Challenge yourself to identify the noncatastrophic thought; for instance, "I may not know these people, but I have a chance to meet new people and learn new things."

The Catastrophic Thinking Chart		
Situation	**Catastrophic thought**	**Noncatastrophic thought**
_____	_____	_____
_____	_____	_____
_____	_____	_____
_____	_____	_____
_____	_____	_____

Weigh the Evidence

If you have assumptions about being alone in the world or being entirely misunderstood, dispute those thoughts with the Disputation Chart. (Examples are provided to assist you.)

The Disputation Chart
Situation: *You are alone at a party.*
Belief: *Because I am alone, I have no one.*

Proof Supporting Belief	Refuting Statement
1. *I have no one with me.*	1. *I have friends and family.*
2. *I don't know anyone.*	2. *I have met strangers who became friends.*
3. _____	3. _____
4. _____	4. _____
5. _____	5. _____
6. _____	6. _____

WORKSHEET 13
Behavioral Triggers

What specific behaviors did you engage in before, during, and after you experienced emptiness? Were you in a group of people and suddenly felt as though you should leave, like the character Tom? Were you alone when you felt this way? Were you bored?

Before:

Behavior 1 _____.

Behavior 2 _____.

Behavior 3 _____.

During:

Behavior 1 _____.

Behavior 2 _____.

Behavior 3 _____.

After:

Behavior 1 _____.

Behavior 2 _____.

Behavior 3 _____.

Detail as much information regarding your behaviors as possible. Use the lines below.

_____

_____

_____

_____

_____

_____

_____

_____

_____

_____

_____

WORKSHEET 14
Behavioral Triggers & Suggested Interventions

Scan the list you just made and identify which specific behaviors you wish to address.

Behavior 1 _____.

Behavior 2 _____.

Behavior 3 _____.

The following interventions can help you alter your behaviors in response to experiencing emptiness.

Consider the Consequences

When experiencing feelings of emptiness, you might not stop to consider the consequences of behaviors that you engage in to combat the emptiness. Look at the behaviors you just listed. What would be the negative and positive consequences of doing them again? For example, Tom choose to leave the group because he felt he had nothing to contribute. The positive consequence was that he no longer had to feel embarrassed or "put on the spot." However, he forfeited his chance to get to know other people or even practice being in a conversation and letting people get to know him.

The Negative and Positive Consequences Chart		
Behavior	**Negative consequences**	**Positive consequences**
_____.	_____.	_____.
_____.	_____.	_____.
_____.	_____.	_____.
_____.	_____.	_____.
_____.	_____.	_____.

After completing the chart, ask yourself the following:

- Do the negative consequences outweigh the positive consequences?
- Is it worth it to decrease this behavior?
- Do I want to continue this behavior?

Stop

Take a moment to stop. If you begin to experience the feeling of emptiness, the thoughts that accompany that feeling may only make you feel additionally tense and distressed. These distressed feelings can often lead you to engage in behaviors you may later regret. When your first experience emptiness, take a moment to stop. This will allow you to consider options before you proceed.

As soon as I experience _____ I should take a moment to stop.

WORKSHEET 16
Situational Triggers

There may be times, individuals, events, and places that seem to trigger your feelings of emptiness. Knowing which situations cause you difficulty can help you be prepared if a similar situation occurs; in particular, you can be on alert for you alarms. You identified your four areas of warning signs in WORKSHEET 3: THE INCIDENT CHART. Now list the situations in which you typically feel isolated, alone, and empty. Is it with large groups of people? Your family? At work? Is it when you are around others that you don't know or are just meeting? Perhaps when you are feeling especially stressed or tired? Review WORKSHEET 1 if you need help identifying these situations.

1. _____

_____

_____.

2. _____

_____

_____.

3. _____

_____

_____.

4. _____

_____

_____.

5. _____

_____

_____.

6. _____

_____

_____.

WORKSHEET 17
Situational Triggers & Suggested Interventions

WORKSHEET 16 identifies those situations in which you have experienced feeling empty. If you are in a situation similar to or included in that list, the following interventions can help you avoid or manage feeling empty.

Remove Yourself

For those situations that you have identified as triggering feelings of emptiness, remember, you can always remove yourself from this type of situation. For example, if you are in a situation in which you are feeling unsure, confused, or overwhelmed with not fitting in, feeling empty, or not knowing how to react, by removing yourself you reinforce that you do have unique needs and emotional states.

When things get particularly difficult, I can _____

_____

_____

_____

_____

_____

_____

_____ .

Try Something Different

For those situations that you identified as triggering feelings of emptiness, try something different in the situation. For example, instead of scanning the room looking for topics of discussion from other party-goers, try to make a statement related to an area of your interests, such as a recent book you read or a movie you've seen.

Instead of _____ [*behavior*],

I can try _____

_____

_____

_____

_____

_____

_____ .

Your therapist will help you complete this worksheet.

FREEMAN DIAGNOSTIC PROFILING SYSTEM
(© FREEMAN, 2003) REVISED EDITION

Date of Assessment: _____

Session#: _____ Evaluator: _____

Patient Name: _____ Patient#: _____ Location: _____

Birthdate: _____ Age: _____ Race: _____ Gender: _____ Birthorder: _____ Marital/Children: _____

Employment: _____ Education: _____ Disability: _____ Medication: _____

Physician: _____ Referral Question: _____

Instructions: Record the diagnosis including the code number. Briefly identify the criteria for the selected diagnosis. Working with the patient either directly as as part of the data gathering of the clinical interview, SCALE the SEVERITY of EACH CRITERION for the patient at the PRESENT TIME. Indicate the level of severity on the grid.

DIAGNOSIS (DSM/ICD) with Code:

Axis I: _____

Axis II: _____

Axis III: _____

SEVERITY OF SYMPTOMS (HIGH / MEDIUM / LOW, scale 1–10)

DESCRIPTIVE CRITERIA (scale 0–12)

CRITERIA:

1 _____ 7 _____

2 _____ 8 _____

3 _____ 9 _____

4 _____ 10 _____

5 _____ 11 _____

6 _____ 12 _____

Do you believe that the above noted criteria are a reaonably accurate sample of the patient's behavior? **YES** or **NO**

If **NO**, please indicate why: _____

Are there any reasons to believe that this individual is an imminent danger to himself/herself or others? **YES** or **NO**

If **YES**, please indicate the danger: _____

(From Freeman, 1998.)

CHALLENGING WHAT YOU KNOW & DO: TAKING CONTROL

As emptiness itself is a difficult concept to define, you might be having a hard time putting into words how this feeling actually presents itself. If you look at the context of how and when you experience emptiness, and then turn up your sensors, you can discover parts of yourself you may not have been reading. Perhaps your schemas are related to avoiding emotions and feelings in order to protect yourself. You also might have identified why your feelings are not always accessible. Perhaps you believe that it is not acceptable to be emotional or that to experience emotions will always be painful. You might fear what will happen if you really do feel. The key is that you *do* feel and you *do* exist. You also have meaning in your life. Whatever your schemas may be, challenge your belief that you are an empty shell or void of meaning.

CHAPTER 8

Seeing Red: Keeping Your Cool

Your sensitivity, concern, and high energy might be seen by others as intense. This intensity at times may even have been frightening to other people. Perhaps there are times when you react by losing your cool. These reactions might be in response to thinking someone is violating your rights as an individual, humiliating you, or actually harming you physically.

As children, we're taught to moderate or control our responses and behaviors. We're taught not to hit when we become angry; we should try to "work things out." We're given direction by family members about how to handle our anger. These directions are then reinforced in our first social experiences in school. Some of us, however, have difficulty knowing when we are getting angry. We might not know when we're about to "blow our stack" or when we have reached our limit. We might then be surprised that our response is considered unacceptable to society.

Do you lose your cool? Friends and family members may have described you as often "hot under the collar" or being "uptight." You might have noticed that your feelings of anger seem to be an overreaction to the actual situation; and afterward you might feel ashamed, embarrassed, or regretful of some of the things you said or did. In severe situations, you may have become physical—throwing objects, hitting, slapping, or punching another person, or placing someone else at risk (e.g., locking someone out of his or her home). These explosions rarely have a positive outcome, but they serve to discharge large amounts of energy, what may feel like a lifetime of pent-up emotions. It is a normal function of being human to experience anger. However, you need to examine whether your anger has become problematic for you.

VIGNETTES

Vignette 1: Kenny

Kenny was getting really annoyed with his wife. She seemed to nag him constantly about his not working. This time he had admitted that he hadn't completed a job he was hired to do and had lost a valuable contract. Yeah, he knew he had screwed up, but her nagging wasn't helping. "How are we supposed to pay the bills?" she asked him. "Who's going to pay the rent?" She just wouldn't let up. "I wish I never married a bitch like you!" Kenny yelled as he stormed out. As he drove around town, her irritating voice played over and over in his head. The last straw came when some idiot in a station wagon cut him off when switching lanes. Kenny saw red. He was unable to feel anything but rage. He tapped the other driver's rear bumper just to let him know how angry he was. What he didn't anticipate was the other drivers' slamming on his breaks.

Vignette 2: Carrie

Carrie was getting annoyed. Sipping her third glass of red wine over dinner, she was becoming infuriated with her friend, Jean's, constant chattering. Jean was laughing and talking about other people, but Carrie thought it seemed to pertain directly to her. Jean talked about her other friend's jobs, clothes, and backgrounds. Carrie's mind raced back to this morning, when she had stood in front of the mirror for at least an hour trying to fit into some of her good clothes. Didn't Jean know that she was feeling incredibly bad about herself right now? "If she cuts up other people that way, what does she think of me?" Carrie thought. She couldn't stand it any longer. She was furious. Tightness welled up in her throat and she felt like she couldn't breathe. She didn't think she could contain herself any longer. Jean was amazed when Carrie tossed what was left of her wine in her face and stormed out of the restaurant.

Review the Vignettes

Do either of these scenarios seem familiar? Kenny and Carrie both became overwhelmed with their feelings of anger and acted in ways that they probably regretted later. Both strongly identified with what other people were saying to them; so much so that whatever good thoughts or feelings they had about themselves or the other person became irrelevant. Their anger became like a runaway train. Any kind of control they may have once had was no longer available to them.

Note the warning signs both received prior to their explosions. Kenny, driving around very irritated and frustrated, kept hearing his wife's voice in his mind. Carrie noted tightness in her throat, low self-esteem, and the feeling that she couldn't contain herself. Both experienced loud warning signs indicating that they were very angry. How else could they have handled their anger? Were they destined to explode?

WHAT YOU WOULD LIKE TO CHANGE

First discuss with your therapist whether this seems to be an area that is problematic for you. Do you relate to the vignettes? Does this behavior appear to occur in a pattern? Is it an area of your life over which you wish you had more control? If it does not seem pertinent, discuss with your therapist whether you need to continue to the assessment section.

SELF-MONITORING: HOW DO I KNOW WHAT MY PERCEPTIONS ARE?

Particularly important to managing your temper outbursts is learning when you are angry. By activating your alarm system, you can begin to watch yourself and, if the alarms go off, choose what type of reaction you want to have. You might often have found yourself extremely enraged and yet not know how you managed to become so angry. You might even feel as if you have no control over your anger. Anger has many potential negative outcomes. But by identifying when you get angry and monitoring your alarm signals, can learn how to manage your anger in a healthy and adaptive way.

Let's look at your anger in two different ways. First, "seeing red" involves the part of you that becomes angry, the part that interprets or "senses" situations and how they apply to you. In both of the scenarios, Kenny and Carrie became enraged at what others were saying to them. They seemed to lose track of their own sense of what mattered to them. This involved their perception of the situation and what others did or said; in other words, how they interpreted others' remarks and applied them to themselves.

Second, how you respond to your anger can either fuel it or put the flames out. How can you learn to take control of your anger? To begin with, it is important that you are able to recognize when you are getting angry. Often, strong physiological clues will indicate that you are getting angry. Perhaps you have felt tightness, tension, or stiff muscles. You also might have experienced extreme emotions related to anger. Perhaps you may have had "tunnel vision" and only thought of what was triggering your anger. All of these signs and symptoms are available for you to read. Therefore, you can make decisions about how you want to handle them.

THE WORKSHEETS

The following section includes several worksheets that address the current chapter topic. The worksheets are designed to help you learn more about yourself so that you can decide if there is anything you wish to change. Your therapist can help you use them.

WORKSHEET 1
The Assessment

Rate the severity of the following problems as you think they may relate to you.

0 = none   1 = mild   2 = moderate   3 = severe   4 = extremely severe

1. You lose your temper easily. ___

2. People have described you as an "angry person." ___

3. You have regretted things you've said in arguments. ___

4. You have used physical force when you argue. ___

5. During arguments your voice gets loud. ___

6. You feel completely out of control when you are angry. ___

7. When you're annoyed, your feel tightness in your chest and your muscles seem tense. ___

8. You find it difficult to think of anything else when you are angry. ___

9. Your anger has gotten you in trouble. ___

10. Others are frightened of your anger. ___

If you have identified yourself as having the tendency to lose your cool, you now have some options. You have the opportunity to handle your anger in a healthy way and learn how to manage your anger from becoming so intense that you end up feeling bad. You also have the option of not controlling your anger and paying a huge price for losing your temper.

WORKSHEET 2
The Assignment

Sit back, relax, and try to think of the last time you experienced feelings of intense rage. You might have realized the anger you felt was an inappropriate reaction to the situation. You might of done things that you later regretted in response to your anger. You might have had a fight with someone and ended up saying something that hurt the other person. Perhaps you have even struck another person. Use the lines below to detail your experience. Be as specific as possible. You will compile your reactions in WORKSHEET 3: THE INCIDENT CHART.

_____

_____

_____

_____

_____

_____

_____

_____

_____

_____

_____

_____

_____

_____

_____

_____

_____

_____

_____

WORKSHEET 3
The Incident Chart*

This worksheet will help you begin uncovering the schema related to this characteristic. Think about the situation you described in WORKSHEET 2 and ask yourself the following:

- What was I physically experiencing before, during, and after the situation?
- What was I feeling?
- What thoughts were running through my mind before, during, and after the situation?
- How was I behaving? [*name some specific behaviors*]

Now fill out the worksheet in as much detail as possible.

Situation: _____

_____.

Prior to Incident

Physiological sensations	Emotions	Cognitions/ thoughts	Behaviors
_____.	_____.	_____.	_____.
_____.	_____.	_____.	_____.
_____.	_____.	_____.	_____.
_____.	_____.	_____.	_____.

During Incident

Physiological sensations	Emotions	Cognitions/ thoughts	Behaviors
_____.	_____.	_____.	_____.
_____.	_____.	_____.	_____.
_____.	_____.	_____.	_____.
_____.	_____.	_____.	_____.

After Incident

Physiological sensations	Emotions	Cognitions/ thoughts	Behaviors
_____.	_____.	_____.	_____.
_____.	_____.	_____.	_____.
_____.	_____.	_____.	_____.
_____.	_____.	_____.	_____.

*(Adapted from J. S. Beck, *Cognitive Therapy: Basics and Beyond*. Guilford Press, 1995©.)

WORKSHEET 4
The DTR*

This worksheet is designed to assist you in identifying your automatic thoughts. Noting your automatic thoughts can help you determine what underlying schemas or beliefs relate to particular events or situations. What are your automatic thoughts related to your anger and expressing your anger? For example, do you experience thoughts such as "My anger is the only way I can really express myself" or "I have no control of myself when I'm angry"? Your therapist will help you with the rest.

Date/Time	Situation	Automatic thought	Emotion	Adaptive response	Outcome

*(Adapted from J. S. Beck, *Cognitive Therapy: Basics and Beyond*. Guilford Press, 1995©.)

WORKSHEET 5
Schemas

What are your rules or schemas related to your anger? Take a moment to write them down.

_____

_____

_____

_____

_____

_____

_____

Choose any of the specific rules and fill in each of the columns. Indicate what the rule is, where (or whom) it comes from, what meaning it has for you, and how likely or easy it would be to change that rule. Once you have identified your particular schemas, how strong they are, and whether or not they can be changed, you can begin to create treatment goals.

Schema	Where it comes from	Meaning to me	Easy to change?

WORKSHEET 6
Treatment Goals

This worksheet asks you to identify your treatment goals, the symptoms that prevent you from obtaining your goals, the schemas that are associated with those goals, and the change that you are hoping for. Are you able to imagine yourself completing the goals? Complete this chart with the help of your therapist and prioritize the importance of each of these goals.

	Symptoms that prevent you from obtaining goal	Schema associated with goal	Hoped-for change	Realistic or unrealistic?	How outcome looks if goal is reached
Goal 1: **Highest priority**					
Goal 2: **High priority**					
Goal 3: **Moderate priority**					
Goal 4: **Low priority**					

WORKSHEET 18
The DPS

Your therapist will help you complete this worksheet.

Date of Assessment: _____

FREEMAN DIAGNOSTIC PROFILING SYSTEM
(© FREEMAN, 2003) REVISED EDITION

Session#: _____ Evaluator: _____

Patient Name: _____ Patient#: _____ Location: _____

Birthdate: _____ Age: _____ Race: _____ Gender: _____ Birthorder: _____ Marital/Children: _____

Employment: _____ Education: _____ Disability: _____ Medication: _____

Physician: _____ Referral Question: _____

Instructions: Record the diagnosis including the code number. Briefly identify the criteria for the selected diagnosis. Working with the patient either directly as as part of the data gathering of the clinical interview, SCALE the SEVERITY of EACH CRITERION for the patient at the PRESENT TIME. Indicate the level of severity on the grid.

DIAGNOSIS (DSM/ICD) with Code:

Axis I: _____

Axis II: _____

Axis III: _____

SEVERITY OF SYMPTOMS — HIGH / MEDIUM / LOW, scale 1–10 on vertical axis, 0–12 on horizontal axis

DESCRIPTIVE CRITERIA

CRITERIA:

1 _____   7 _____

2 _____   8 _____

3 _____   9 _____

4 _____   10 _____

5 _____   11 _____

6 _____   12 _____

Do you believe that the above noted criteria are a reaonably accurate sample of the patient's behavior? **YES** or **NO**

If **NO**, please indicate why: _____

Are there any reasons to believe that this individual is an imminent danger to himself/herself or others? **YES** or **NO**

If **YES**, please indicate the danger: _____

(From Freeman, 1998.)

WORKSHEET 7
Physical Triggers

Physical sensations are clues to help you avoid future distressful situations. The physical signs and symptoms of rage often occur in exaggerated forms. They are a very predictable aspect of anger. By identifying your physical warning signs of anger, you can begin to take steps to divert your anger or handle it in a way you won't later regret. Think of the experience you described in WORKSHEET 2: THE ASSIGNMENT. What were you physically experiencing before, during, and after you became enraged? You might have felt some of the following:

- queasy stomach.
- sweating/clammy skin.
- racing heart.
- tension.
- GI distress.

Use the lines below to describe your physical sensations.

_____

_____

_____

_____

_____

_____

_____

_____

_____

_____

_____

_____

_____

_____

_____

_____

_____

WORKSHEET 8
Physical Triggers & Suggested Interventions

This area of intervention is especially important when you are trying to handle anger. Once your warning signs have gone off, you can attempt to "turn your body down" by trying the following: (1) take a moment to stop; (2) employ relaxation techniques; and (3) use relaxing imagery.

Stop

In WORKSHEET 4, you identified the thoughts directly related to intense anger. For this exercise, identify the thoughts that seem to be creating or exacerbating uncomfortable physical reactions. Use the lines below to write down those thoughts.

_____

_____

_____

_____

If you have read your body's signals that you are becoming angry, take a moment to stop. This will allow you to consider options before you proceed.

As soon as I experience _____ I should take a moment to stop.

Relax

In WORKSHEET 3, you identified what specific physical symptoms occur when you are becoming angry or enraged. If you know what physical symptoms are related to feeling angry, you can utilize relaxation techniques when you experience those symptoms. Relaxation techniques will ease your body's tension-filled state.

You can do this by _____

_____

_____

_____

Relaxing Imagery

When imagining your safe place, be sure to try to block out anything that could remotely add to your anger.

I feel safe imagining _____

_____

_____

_____

I hear _____

_____

_____

_____.

I feel _____

_____

_____

_____.

I can see _____

_____

_____

_____.

I can smell _____

_____

_____

_____.

I can taste _____

_____

_____

_____.

My safe person who can join me here is _____

_____

_____

_____.

WORKSHEET 9
Emotional Triggers

How would you describe the emotions you had when you were enraged? Were you experiencing some type of humiliation or some type of sadness? Use WORKSHEETS 3 and 4 to identify some of the feelings you had when you were enraged. They might include some of the following:

- fear.
- anger.
- sadness.
- disgust.

What were you feeling emotionally? Write down what those feelings were like.

_____

_____

_____

_____

_____

_____

_____

_____

_____

_____

_____

_____

_____

_____

_____

_____

_____

WORKSHEET 10
Emotional Triggers & Suggested Interventions

As you are probably very psychologically sensitive, feelings of anger and rage can be unbearable. It may feel as if you have no control over the rage building inside you, and that you are a victim of your own painful emotional states. As a reaction to these very painful emotional states, you might do or say things you regret later on.

Scale Back

Pick one of the uncomfortable emotional responses (or anger itself) you wish to address from WORKSHEET 9. On a scale of 1 to 10 (1 being least severe and 10 being most severe), rate the severity of the emotion you experienced when you experienced anger.

   1   2   3   4   5   6   7   8   9   10

As you continue to have uncomfortable emotions related to your anger (or continue being angry), try to scale back or "turn the oven down." You might want to combine scaling back with some relaxation techniques described in WORKSHEET 8 on physical triggers. Once you have turned yourself down, rate your emotions again.

   1   2   3   4   5   6   7   8   9   10

How did you do? Were you able to turn yourself down? You'll notice that with practice, turning down your own emotional temperature becomes easier and easier. Can you describe how you are feeling now?

_____

_____

_____

_____

_____

_____

_____

_____

_____

_____

_____

_____

_____

_____ .

WORKSHEET 11
Cognitive/Automatic Thoughts

What thoughts were running through your mind before, during, and after you became enraged? Identifying these is particularly important, as your assumptions and ongoing thoughts in response to your bodily sensations tend fuel your anger. For example, when you become enraged, do you experience thoughts such as "I can't help what I do when I'm angry" or "I have no control of my anger"? Refer to WORKSHEET 4: THE DTR to help identify the specific thoughts related to this topic. Write your responses below.

_____

_____

_____

_____

_____

_____

_____

_____

_____

_____

_____

_____

_____

_____

_____

_____

_____

_____

_____

_____.

WORKSHEET 12
Cognitive/Automatic Thoughts & Suggested Interventions

Rage emotions and reactions are often generated from misread or misinterpreted cues. (Remember Whisper Down the Lane?) You might have experienced what someone else has said or did as something that upsets and angers you. There are times when it is appropriate to be angry. However, if you have a tendency to act out of rage, there is a high likelihood that you are changing the original message and reacting to the distortions of your own biased system.

Consider the thoughts that seem to fuel your anger. Are they related to anger toward the other person or to something negative about yourself? Were you assuming you were being left or abandoned? Were you engaging in catastrophic or black-and-white thinking?

Utilize WORKSHEET 15: THE EXPANDED INCIDENT CHART (pp. 213–216). This worksheet can help you define the context of your anger. Be sure to write down the specific situations and people that seem to trigger you.

WORKSHEET 15
The Expanded Incident Chart

As you complete this worksheet, ask yourself the following:

- What was I physically experiencing before, during, and after the situation?
- What was I feeling?
- What thoughts were running through my mind before, during, and after the situation?
- How was I behaving? [*name some specific behaviors*]
- Is there a specific person or group associated with this situation?

Situation: _____.

Prior to Incident

People	Physiological sensations	Emotions	Cognitions/ thoughts	Behaviors
_____.	_____.	_____.	_____.	_____
_____.	_____.	_____.	_____.	_____

During Incident

People	Physiological sensations	Emotions	Cognitions/ thoughts	Behaviors
_____.	_____.	_____.	_____.	_____
_____.	_____.	_____.	_____.	_____

After Incident

People	Physiological sensations	Emotions	Cognitions/ thoughts	Behaviors
_____.	_____.	_____.	_____.	_____
_____.	_____.	_____.	_____.	_____

Use the Anger Chain

Let's look at how you view situations. The flowchart below can help you understand how you interpret an event or argument in a way that creates tension and anger for you. Your response to anger follows by a chain of events. This chain of events usually begins with a distorted or negative perception of a situation. Vital in this process is your making a decision: Do I wish to change how I react? Do you want to alter the chain of events that leads you to act out of rage? In other words, do you wish to make a conscious choice to change how you handle anger? The ANGER CHAIN will help you follow how your initial perceptions can lead you to have rage reactions or respond to your rage in an inappropriate way.

> **The Anger Chain**
>
> 1. Perception of event (physiologically through senses).
> 2. Schematic interpretation.
> 3. Application to self.
> 4. Chain of events triggered.
> 5. Physiological responses.
> 6. Increased internal pressure.
> 7. Anger response to relieve pressure (short-term solution!)

Let's look at each of these components individually. The following sections define the components of the chain and provide suggestions to counter the chain of events that occurs when you become angry. Remember that each stage holds opportunities for you to change your response.

Perception of Event

What is our physical warning system perceiving? How do you typically perceive something?

Challenge Perceptions

Try to challenge what you think you are perceiving. Ask yourself, "Is this really happening?" or "Is it likely that I'm really seeing what I think I'm seeing?"

Weigh the Evidence

What is the actual likelihood that what you are perceiving is true? (Examples are provided to assist you.)

The Disputation Chart

Situation: *Friend yawns when I'm talking to her.*

Belief: *My friend thinks I'm not important.*

Proof Supporting Belief	**Refuting Statement**
1. *Friend's yawn means I bore her.*	1. *Friend could be tired.*
2. *Friend is disrespectful to me.*	2. *Friend is usually interested in what I say.*
3. _____ .	3. _____ .
4. _____ .	4. _____ .
5. _____ .	5. _____ .
6. _____ .	6. _____ .

Schematic Interpretation

The senses send complicated messages to the brain, which interprets the data. Your schemas help you organize the world. How does your perceived information get interpreted?

Challenge Black-and-White Thinking

Use your artist's palette.

The Dichotomous Thinking Chart

Black	**Gray(s)**	**White**
	--	--	
Rage.	*I can be annoyed and still care for someone.*	*Happy.*
Relationship is over.	*Conflict is normal in relationships.*	*Relationship is safe.*
_____ .	_____ .	_____ .
_____ .	_____ .	_____ .
_____ .	_____ .	_____ .
_____ .	_____ .	_____ .

Common-Sense Questions

Ask yourself some common-sense questions such as "Does this really make sense?" or "Is this really likely to happen?"

Reflect on Previous Experiences

Have there been times when you have made similar assumptions, only to discover later you were very wrong? Is this situation similar?

Application to Self

Different pieces of information mean different things to us. A stranger approaching us on a dark street might make us fearful, whereas a friend approaching us in an office probably doesn't. We interpret things in a pattern based on many years of experience. This pattern is a part of who we are and how we react as adults. Do you tend to interpret things personally? Once you've made an interpretation, try to look outside your own experience and make a realistic assumption about the situation.

Chain of Events Triggered

As the incoming information is processed through your schemas, many bits of information become linked. We associate certain parts of the environment with other parts. For instance, if we see a stranger approaching us, it might not necessarily scare us. But when we pair this with being alone and in a dark place, our alarm system activates a fear response. We then react accordingly to what we have interpreted as a dangerous situation. Again, how we react to a situation is based upon experience. What has worked well in the past? What is likely to occur if you react in a certain way? All of these components are added into the mixture as you decide how to react.

Break the Chain of Events

Once the chain of events begins with a trigger, thoughts and emotions are generated. These thoughts and emotions lead to subsequent physiological responses and ultimately behaviors. How can you break the chain of events?

Physiological Responses

As we interpret the information presented to us, our body begins to react. In the case of the stranger approaching us in a dark alley, we might feel our heartbeat increase, we may have trouble swallowing, and our muscles may become very tense. This is usually an exaggeration of the initial physical sensations we might have felt. When we become angry, similar responses occur. Our heartrate might speed up, we can feel "knotted up" inside, and we can experience an overall bodily tension that normally doesn't exist.

Relax

Use relaxation exercises to counter these physical responses.

Increased Internal Pressure

As we continue to feel and become aware of how our body is reacting, a negative loop is established. As we get more angry, our body becomes more tense; as we get more tense, we become more angry.

Decrease the Pressure

Once you identify that pressure is building, you can choose to break the chain by attempting to decrease it. Like a pressure cooker on a stove, you need to identify ways in which to release the steam and cool off. Use the scaling back exercise.

Avoid the Situation

List the places or people that encourage your anger-related behaviors. Create an "escape hatch" or "safe place" that you can go to when you become overwhelmed or angered.

Anger Response to Relieve Pressure

In an effort to release the internal frustration and pressure, we react. Just like a pressure cooker, your body seeks to relieve itself by eliminating the pent-up emotions. You might decide to lash out at whomever seems to be causing the incredible internal pressure. You might even lash out at yourself by harming yourself. Perhaps you will scream, punch, hit, throw objects, or create dangerous situations for those around you. It doesn't need to happen this way. How do you react? If you respond impulsively or out of anger, it only provides a short-term solution to the problem.

Consider the Consequences

Complete the following chart; examples are provided to assist you.

The Negative and Positive Consequences Chart		
Behavior *Yelling at person.* *Throwing something.*	**Negative consequences** *Distancing and frightening the person.* *Harming someone or something.*	**Positive consequences** *Release of tension.* *Getting my point across.*
_____ .	_____ .	_____ .
_____ .	_____ .	_____ .
_____ .	_____ .	_____ .
_____ .	_____ .	_____ .
_____ .	_____ .	_____ .
_____ .	_____ .	_____ .
_____ .	_____ .	_____ .

After completing the chart, ask yourself the following:

- Do the negative consequences outweigh the positive consequences?
- Is it worth it to decrease this behavior?
- Do I want to continue this behavior?

WORKSHEET 13
Behavioral Triggers

What specific behaviors did you engage in before, during, and after you became enraged? Do you traditionally argue or yell? Were you trying to prove a point or convince someone of something? Were you defending yourself? What did you do as a reaction to your rage; yell, scream, punch walls, or shake your fist?

Before:

Behavior 1 _____.

Behavior 2 _____.

Behavior 3 _____.

During:

Behavior 1 _____.

Behavior 2 _____.

Behavior 3 _____.

After:

Behavior 1 _____.

Behavior 2 _____.

Behavior 3 _____.

Detail as much information regarding your behaviors as possible. Use the lines below.

_____

_____

_____

_____

_____

_____

_____

_____

_____

_____

WORKSHEET 14
Behavioral Triggers & Suggested Interventions

Scan the list you just made and identify which specific behaviors you wish to address.

Behavior 1 _____.

Behavior 2 _____.

Behavior 3 _____.

There are many ways you can release pent-up energy. You could use that energy to complete a project you've been meaning to finish. You could exercise. Try to think of some ways you can release your angry energy.

Rather than doing _____ [*behavior*],

next time I will try to _____

_____

_____

_____

_____

_____

_____

_____

_____

_____

_____

_____.

WORKSHEET 16
Situational Triggers

There may be times, individuals, events, and places that seem to trigger your feelings of anger. Knowing which situations cause you difficulty can help you be prepared if a similar situation occurs; in particular, you can be on alert for your alarms. You identified your four areas of warning signs in WORKSHEET 2: THE ASSIGNMENT. Now list the situations in which you have experienced difficulty keeping your cool. For example, do you become irritable if you drink? Are there particular people or places that seem to trigger your anger? Particular times or situations? Review WORKSHEET 1 if you need help identifying these situations.

1. _____

   _____

   _____.

2. _____

   _____

   _____.

3. _____

   _____

   _____.

4. _____

   _____

   _____.

5. _____

   _____

   _____.

6. _____

   _____

   _____.

WORKSHEET 17
Situational Triggers & Suggested Interventions

WORKSHEET 16 identifies those situations in which you have experienced rage or intense anger. If you are in a situation similar to or included in that list, the following interventions can help you avoid or manage your anger.

Remove Yourself

For those situations that you identified as triggering intense anger or rage, remember that you can always remove yourself from this type of situation. For example, if you are in a situation in which you are feeling angered, instead of allowing yourself to lose control, removing yourself can prevent doing something you may later regret.

When things get particularly difficult, I can _____

_____

_____

_____

_____

_____

_____

_____ .

Try Something Different

Is there something else you can try? What else could you do? For example, instead of throwing something out of anger, could you go for a walk? Call a friend?

Instead of _____ [*behavior*],

I can try _____

_____

_____

_____

_____

_____

_____

_____ .

The DPS

Your therapist will help you complete this worksheet.

FREEMAN DIAGNOSTIC PROFILING SYSTEM
(© FREEMAN, 2003) REVISED EDITION

Date of Assessment: _____

Session#: _____ Evaluator: _____

Patient Name: _____ Patient#: _____ Location: _____

Birthdate: _____ Age: _____ Race: _____ Gender: _____ Birthorder: _____ Marital/Children: _____

Employment: _____ Education: _____ Disability: _____ Medication: _____

Physician: _____ Referral Question: _____

Instructions: Record the diagnosis including the code number. Briefly identify the criteria for the selected diagnosis. Working with the patient either directly as as part of the data gathering of the clinical interview, SCALE the SEVERITY of EACH CRITERION for the patient at the PRESENT TIME. Indicate the level of severity on the grid.

DIAGNOSIS (DSM/ICD) with Code:

Axis I: _____

Axis II: _____

Axis III: _____

SEVERITY OF SYMPTOMS (HIGH / MEDIUM / LOW, 1–10)

DESCRIPTIVE CRITERIA (0–12)

CRITERIA:

1 _____   7 _____

2 _____   8 _____

3 _____   9 _____

4 _____   10 _____

5 _____   11 _____

6 _____   12 _____

Do you believe that the above noted criteria are a reasonably accurate sample of the patient's behavior? **YES** or **NO**

If **NO**, please indicate why: _____

Are there any reasons to believe that this individual is an imminent danger to himself/herself or others? **YES** or **NO**

If **YES**, please indicate the danger: _____

(From Freeman, 1998.)

CHALLENGING WHAT YOU KNOW & DO: TAKING CONTROL

Consider where you have learned your beliefs about anger. Do you believe you are able to control it? Again, by remaining focused on identifying how your system reacts, you can control your anger by directing its energy toward something that will benefit you rather than potentially harm you. The key is that you remain aware of the connections your own system makes that exacerbate your anger. You do not have to continue losing your cool. The cycle of the creation and maintenance of angry outbursts offers many opportunities for intervention. Remember, you have a choice about how to handle your anger. The energy that you are presently putting into containing your anger, being angry, and then feeling bad about your anger can be put to better use, ultimately making you more productive and happier. The key is to examine what you are saying to yourself more than what you hear other people saying to you.

CHAPTER 9

Suspicion: Who Can I Trust?

Stress occurs for everyone on a daily basis. It can come from external and internal sources. External stressors can be our job, bills, difficult relationships, or even the traffic. Internal stressors can be negative feelings we have about ourselves, pressure we place on ourselves to do things a certain way, or feelings of inadequacy. Stress can also be cumulative, gathering in our system and slowly wearing us down.

In times of extreme stress, sensitive people can react in many ways. You might act impulsively in an attempt to decrease the tension. Perhaps you withdraw or isolate yourself from others. Soon you might feel that because so many bad things seem to happen to you, you are being singled out. In the context of relationships, you can feel singled out and fear that significant others are rejecting or leaving *you*. You might become vigilant for signs of disloyalty; extreme sensitivity to pending loss combined with stressful situations might lead you to feel that significant others are unreliable if not deceitful.

In response to your fears, you might take steps to prevent harm from occurring by protecting yourself. Perhaps you isolate yourself. You might lash out at others in response to your own fear and suspiciousness. These feelings are uncomfortable and tend to absorb your each and every thought. They can be exhausting. These feelings tend to be short-lived and they usually subside when loved ones reassure you that they are not leaving or trying to inflict harm.

Do you feel as if others might not be acting in your best interest? Do you sometimes become convinced that others want to hurt or harm you? Keep one thing in mind—your internal alarm system can become activated not only during inappropriate times, but also during appropriate times. In other words, there are times when it is vital for you to be suspicious, and there are times when it is *not* appropriate. These latter instances are the ones you should consider. Often, reactions that occur from these feelings of suspiciousness prompt us to act or think in ways that are not beneficial to us. These actions might lead to later embarrassment and place additional strain on our relationships and interactions with others.

VIGNETTES

Vignette 1: Kim

Kim was tired. She had been working double shifts at the diner just to make the bills this month. When would it all end? When she returned to her apartment after a long night of serving greasy burgers, she noticed her boyfriend, Bill, packing items into the back of his truck. Just what did he think he was doing? Her mind raced as she got out of her car. Her heartbeat pounded in her temples. "He's moving out," she thought. "He's leaving me. He's met someone else. Probably some twit he works with at the hospital." Furious and terrified, she ran from her car and yelled, "You bastard, how could you do this to me?" Puzzled by this display of anger, Bill tried to calm her down. She started yelling at him and kicking his tires. While she was taking a breath she noticed that the boxes in his truck were items marked to be distributed to charities.

Vignette 2: Clare

Clare sat at her desk overwhelmed by what seemed to be hundreds of feelings. There was a collection for a baby shower gift for one of the women in the public relations department. Nobody came to collect anything from her. What did that mean? Were they not going to invite her? Did they not even want her name on the card? She felt alternately angry, sad, annoyed, hurt, and vindictive.

"I would really like to get even with them," she thought. She spent the next hour reviewing everything that had transpired between her and the other women in the office. She started to see a pattern emerge. Little slights, minor rebuffs, tiny experiences of being avoided. As she thought about these things it seemed more and more obvious. Clare's heart pounded, her stomach was upset, and she was feeling very jittery. She left her office to get a drink of water.

When Sue came into Clare's office for the third time to collect money for the gift and to have Clare sign the card, she found Clare away from her desk again. As she was leaving she ran into Clare, who blurted out that she would be unable to come to the party and therefore did not think that she would contribute to the gift.

Review the Vignettes

Do either of these scenarios seem familiar to you? In both scenarios the characters are under stress and make assumptions that others are excluding them, leaving them, or trying to harm them in some way. Kim and Clare both automatically jumped to negative conclusions and acted on those suspicious con-

clusions. If you tend to think this way, you might have noticed that you pay very close attention to what others are doing or saying; in times of great stress, you become not only attentive but very guarded. Under stress you need to protect yourself.

Note the character's warning signs. They became very anxious, stressed, and agitated. Kim and Clare also experienced thoughts related to others' not having their best interests in mind; they felt annoyed, angry, and frustrated at what they were experiencing. Kim and Clare made irrational conclusions that affected how their situations turned out. They perceived information through their biased systems which led them to act in ways they later regretted.

WHAT YOU WOULD LIKE TO CHANGE

First discuss with your therapist whether this seems to be an area that is problematic for you. Do you relate to the vignettes? Does this behavior appear to occur in a pattern? Is it an area of your life over which you wish you had more control? If it does not seem pertinent, discuss with your therapist whether you need to continue to the assessment section.

SELF-MONITORING: HOW DO I KNOW WHAT MY PERCEPTIONS ARE?

As a very sensitive person, you probably are highly attuned to the events and situations around you. If you have found that you tend to become suspicious, you might have your sensors on too high. In other words, you can be setting off false alarms. Your system is noting intruders when there might not actually be any.

THE WORKSHEETS

The following section includes several worksheets that address the current chapter topic. The worksheets are designed to help you learn more about yourself so that you can decide if there is anything you wish to change. Your therapist can help you use them.

WORKSHEET 1
The Assessment

Rate the severity of the following problems as you think they may relate to you.

0 = none   1 = mild   2 = moderate   3 = severe   4 = extremely severe

1. If someone close to you doesn't stick to scheduled plans, you assume that it is directly related to how he or she feels about you. ____

2. If someone close to you is late, you assume the worst possible scenario. ____

3. You tend to regret your actions after an argument. ____

4. You tend to jump to conclusions very quickly. ____

5. You tend to be on guard for disloyalty on the part of others. ____

6. You've discovered that you tend to switch emotions very quickly. ____

7. When you disagree with someone, you feel as if he or she not only doesn't agree with you, but also wants to harm you. ____

8. You tend to feel singled out when bad things happen. ____

9. You think that bad things happen to you more often than they happen to others. ____

10. You tend to distrust others when you are stressed. ____

Do you fit this picture? Again, noting that this has been a problem for you is the first step. Often you might have reacted to things and events that you later realized weren't really what they seemed. Perhaps loved ones have not been out to harm you or leave you, but as sensitive as you are, you interpreted situations in a way that activated your alarm system and caused you to begin protecting yourself or reacting in ways you later regretted.

WORKSHEET 2
The Assignment

Think of the last time you experienced feelings of suspicion. You might have realized the suspiciousness was inappropriate for the situation. You might have done things that you later regretted due to this feeling. Try to imagine the buildup of emotions and the running train of thoughts that went through your mind. Use the lines below to detail your experience. Be as specific as possible. You will compile your reactions in WORKSHEET 3: THE INCIDENT CHART.

_____

_____

_____

_____

_____

_____

_____

_____

_____

_____

_____

_____

_____

_____

_____

_____

_____

_____

_____

_____

_____

WORKSHEET 3
The Incident Chart*

This worksheet will help you begin uncovering the schema related to this characteristic. Think about the situation you described in WORKSHEET 2 and ask yourself the following:

- What was I physically experiencing before, during, and after the situation?
- What was I feeling?
- What thoughts were running through my mind before, during, and after the situation?
- How was I behaving? [*name some specific behaviors*]

Now fill out the worksheet in as much detail as possible.

Situation: _____

_____.

Prior to Incident

Physiological sensations	Emotions	Cognitions/ thoughts	Behaviors
_____ .	_____ .	_____ .	_____ .
_____	_____	_____	_____
_____	_____	_____	_____
_____	_____	_____	_____

During Incident

Physiological sensations	Emotions	Cognitions/ thoughts	Behaviors
_____ .	_____ .	_____ .	_____ .
_____	_____	_____	_____
_____	_____	_____	_____
_____ .	_____ .	_____ .	_____ .

After Incident

Physiological sensations	Emotions	Cognitions/ thoughts	Behaviors
_____ .	_____ .	_____ .	_____ .
_____ .	_____ .	_____ .	_____ .
_____ .	_____ .	_____ .	_____ .
_____ .	_____ .	_____ .	_____ .

*(Adapted from J. S. Beck, *Cognitive Therapy: Basics and Beyond*. Guilford Press, 1995©.)

WORKSHEET 4
The DTR*

This worksheet is designed to assist you in identifying your automatic thoughts. Noting you automatic thoughts can help you determine what underlying schemas or beliefs relate to particular events or situations. What are your automatic thoughts related to not trusting others or becoming suspicious? For example, do you experience thoughts such as "If my girlfriend/boyfriend is late, he/she must be unfaithful" or "When my friend forgets to call me, she means to hurt me"? Your therapist will help you with the rest.

Date/Time	Situation	Automatic thought	Emotion	Adaptive response	Outcome

*(Adapted from J. S. Beck, *Cognitive Therapy: Basics and Beyond.* Guilford Press, 1995©.)

WORKSHEET 5
Schemas

What are your rules or schemas related to being suspicious? Take a moment to write them down.

_____

_____

_____

_____

_____

_____

_____.

Choose any of the specific rules and fill in each of the columns. Indicate what the rule is, where (or whom) it comes from, what meaning it has for you, and how likely or easy it would be for you to change that rule. Once you have identified your particular schemas, how strong they are, and whether or not they can be changed, you can begin to create treatment goals.

Schema	Where it comes from	Meaning to me	Easy to change?

WORKSHEET 6
Treatment Goals

This worksheet asks you to identify your treatment goals, the symptoms that prevent you from obtaining your goals, the schemas that are associated with those goals, and the change that you are hoping for. Are you able to imagine yourself completing the goals? Complete this chart with the help of your therapist and prioritize the importance of each of these goals.

	Symptoms that prevent you from obtaining goal	Schema associated with goal	Hoped-for change	Realistic or unrealistic?	How outcome looks if goal is reached
Goal 1: **Highest priority**					
Goal 2: **High priority**					
Goal 3: **Moderate priority**					
Goal 4: **Low priority**					

Your therapist will help you complete this worksheet.

FREEMAN DIAGNOSTIC PROFILING SYSTEM
(© FREEMAN, 2003) REVISED EDITION

Date of Assessment: _____

Session#: _____ Evaluator: _____

Patient Name: _____ Patient#: _____ Location: _____

Birthdate: _____ Age: _____ Race: _____ Gender: _____ Birthorder: _____ Marital/Children: _____

Employment: _____ Education: _____ Disability: _____ Medication: _____

Physician: _____ Referral Question: _____

Instructions: Record the diagnosis including the code number. Briefly identify the criteria for the selected diagnosis. Working with the patient either directly as as part of the data gathering of the clinical interview, SCALE the SEVERITY of EACH CRITERION for the patient at the PRESENT TIME. Indicate the level of severity on the grid.

DIAGNOSIS (DSM/ICD) with Code:

Axis I: _____

Axis II: _____

Axis III: _____

SEVERITY OF SYMPTOMS (vertical axis: HIGH 8–10, MEDIUM 4–7, LOW 1–3, values 1 to 10)

DESCRIPTIVE CRITERIA (horizontal axis: 0 to 12)

CRITERIA:

1 _____   7 _____

2 _____   8 _____

3 _____   9 _____

4 _____   10 _____

5 _____   11 _____

6 _____   12 _____

Do you believe that the above noted criteria are a reaonably accurate sample of the patient's behavior? **YES** or **NO**

If **NO**, please indicate why: _____

Are there any reasons to believe that this individual is an imminent danger to himself/herself or others? **YES** or **NO**

If **YES**, please indicate the danger: _____

(From Freeman, 1998.)

WORKSHEET 7
Physical Triggers

Physical sensations are clues to help you avoid future distressful situations. Your physical warning signs probably will first let you know when you are becoming suspicious. This is largely because, when you become suspicious, people usually are afraid that something or someone will hurt them. The body naturally responds to that fear in what is called the *flight, fright, or freeze response*. Think of the experience you described in WORKSHEET 2: THE ASSIGNMENT. What were you physically experiencing before, during, and after you become suspicious? You might have felt some of the following:

- queasy stomach.
- sweating/clammy skin.
- racing heart.
- tension.
- GI distress.

Use the lines below to describe your physical sensations.

_____

_____

_____

_____

_____

_____

_____

_____

_____

_____

_____

_____

_____

_____

WORKSHEET 8
Physical Triggers & Suggested Interventions

Your physical alarm system might be the first to alert you that you are frightened and potentially suspicious. If you note you are feeling this way, you can give yourself time to really check out the situation by stopping and relaxing. This will give you a chance to consider all of your options. Three techniques can help you combat physiological distress: (1) take a moment to stop; (2) employ relaxation techniques and (3) use relaxing imagery.

Stop

In WORKSHEET 4, you identified the thoughts directly related to your experience of feeling suspicious. For this exercise, identify the thoughts that seem to be creating or exacerbating uncomfortable physical reactions. Use the lines below to write down those thoughts.

_____

_____

_____

_____

_____

Unless you are in immediate danger, stop when you notice your body reacting as if you are afraid. As physical arousal tends to accelerate our runaway thoughts, it is important that you give yourself the chance to look at the situation carefully.

I know I am scared when my body _____

_____

_____

I know I need to stop when I feel _____

_____

_____

Relax

In WORKSHEET 3, you identified what specific physical symptoms occur when you are suspicious. If you know what physical symptoms are related to suspiciousness, you can utilize relaxation techniques when you experience those symptoms. Relaxing is not an easy thing to do if you are scared. However, if you can learn to respond to fear by relaxing, you are in effect counteracting what your body is doing. Your muscles can relax and you therefore can halt the process of thoughts that might or might not be appropriate to the situation.

You can relax by _____

_____

_____

Relaxing Imagery

If you have stopped and started to relax, you can utilize your safe place. Be sure to imagine that you are completely safe where no one can harm you. If you want to imagine someone with you, think of someone you have never been fearful or distrustful of.

I feel safe imagining _____

_____

_____.

I hear _____

_____

_____.

I feel _____

_____

_____.

I can see _____

_____

_____.

I can smell _____

_____

_____.

I can taste _____

_____

_____.

My safe person who can join me here is _____

_____

_____.

WORKSHEET 9
Emotional Triggers

How would you describe that emotions you had when you started to become suspicious? Use WORKSHEETS 3 and 4 to identify some of the feelings you had when you became suspicious. They might include some of the following:

- fear.
- anger.
- sadness.
- disgust.

What were you feeling emotionally? Write down what those feelings were like.

_____

_____

_____

_____

_____

_____

_____

_____

_____

_____

_____

_____

_____

_____

_____

WORKSHEET 10
Emotional Triggers & Suggested Interventions

The following exercises are designed to help you with your emotions. Sometimes emotions become so powerful that decisions are made "from the heart," without thinking. These exercises can help you understand your emotions and how they can impact your decisions.

Scale Back

One of the most obvious emotions that you can experience if you are suspicious is fear. Fear can be felt very strongly; the emotion can even lead to a state of terror. If you are experiencing terror and you are not in a life-threatening situation, try scaling back. After scaling back, do you perceive the situation in the same way?

Pick one of the uncomfortable emotional responses you wish to address from WORKSHEET 9. On a scale of 1 to 10 (1 being least severe and 10 being most severe), rate the severity of the emotion you experienced when you were suspicious.

    1   2   3   4   5   6   7   8   9   10

As you continue to have uncomfortable emotions related to suspicion, try to scale back or "turn the oven down." You may want to combine scaling back with some relaxation techniques described in WORKSHEET 8 on physical triggers. Once you have turned yourself down, rate your emotions again.

    1   2   3   4   5   6   7   8   9   10

How did you do? Were you able to turn yourself down? You'll notice that with practice, turning down your own emotional temperature becomes easier and easier. Can you describe how you are feeling now?

_____

_____

_____

_____

_____

_____

_____

_____

_____

_____

_____

_____

WORKSHEET 11
Cognitive/Automatic Thoughts

Your thoughts will often fuel fears that others might harm you. Perhaps you may have noticed that you tend to jump to conclusions quickly or assume the worst. What thoughts were running through your mind before, during, and after you were suspicious? For example, do you experience thoughts such as "If my husband doesn't agree with me, he's against me" or "When my friend doesn't call me, she has chosen not to invite me out"? Refer to WORKSHEET 4: THE DTR to help identify the specific thoughts related to this topic. Write your responses below.

_____

_____

_____

_____

_____

_____

_____

_____

_____

_____

_____

_____

_____

_____

_____

_____

_____

_____

_____

WORKSHEET 12
Cognitive/Automatic Thoughts & Suggested Interventions

What are your typical thoughts and assumptions? Try challenging those assumptions.

Challenge Catastrophic Thinking

Are you catastrophizing what someone's behavior may be? Do you jump to the worst conclusions? For example, if you have an argument with a friend, do you automatically assume your friend only has the worst intentions for you? Challenge that thought with, "Everyone disagrees about something, it doesn't mean my friend has bad intentions."

The Catastrophic Thinking Chart		
Situation	**Catastrophic thought**	**Noncatastrophic thought**
_____ .	_____ .	_____ .
_____ .	_____ .	_____ .
_____ .	_____ .	_____ .
_____ .	_____ .	_____ .
_____ .	_____ .	_____ .
_____ .	_____ .	_____ .
_____ .	_____ .	_____ .
_____ .	_____ .	_____ .

Some additional suggestions are:

- Ask yourself "What if?" questions.
  Ask yourself, "What if this is true? What if it isn't?"

- Ask yourself "common-sense" questions.
  When you ask yourself "common-sense" questions such as "Could this really be happening?" or "Could I be reading this wrong?" you challenge your beliefs about what you may be perceiving or experiencing.

- Reflect on previous experiences.
  Consider whatever situation is making you feel uncomfortable. Have you been in a similar situation in the past? What was the result of that situation?

Challenge Black-and-White Thinking

Use your artist's palette to mix the grays. What could be causing someone's behaviors besides their wanting to harm you? For example, suppose a friend did not say hello to you in a café. How would you view the situation? (Examples are provided to assist you.)

The Dichotomous Thinking Chart

Black   **Gray(s)**   **White**

|---|---|

She didn't say hello to me in the café,   *She'll chat with me later;*   *She isn't avoiding me.*
so she must be avoiding me.   *She's preoccupied.*

_____ .   _____ .   _____ .

_____ .   _____ .   _____ .

_____ .   _____ .   _____ .

I have a hard time mixing grays related to _____

_____

_____ .

Weigh the Evidence

Are you making assumptions without carefully looking at the evidence? (Examples are provided to assist you.)

The Disputation Chart

Situation: *Friend didn't call as planned.*

Belief: *Friend likes others more than me.*

Proof Supporting Belief   **Refuting Statement**
1. *Friend didn't contact me.*   1. *Friend usually contacts me unless she's busy.*
2. *Friend may be with other friends.*   2. *Friend can go out with others and still like me.*

3. _____ .   3. _____ .

4. _____ .   4. _____ .

5. _____ .   5. _____ .

6. _____ .   6. _____ .

Expanded Incident Chart

Use WORKSHEET 15: THE EXPANDED INCIDENT CHART to detail your chain of thoughts. In addition to asking what are your cognitions, emotions, physiological symptoms, and behaviors, identify the people and situations that seem to trigger your suspiciousness. Keep in mind that your initial interpretation of events leads to your alarm system being activated. Associations are made with the information that is filtered through your sensory system. If you have made a negative association involving external events, people or situations, physiological responses, negative thoughts, reactive behaviors, and emotional upset can occur. When upset, you might perceive that you are no longer in control and that your worst fears are being realized. Feeling as if you have lost control can trigger feelings of paranoia. When one feels out of control, one loses the ability to assert oneself. Perhaps you feel so overwhelmed with emotion that you are unable to clearly express your fears and feelings. In sum, you might become unsure if what you are perceiving is real, or if the information is the product of a learned schema which has led to a patterned response to the situation.

WORKSHEET 15
The Expanded Incident Chart

As you complete this worksheet, ask yourself the following:

- What was I physically experiencing before, during, and after the situation?
- What was I feeling?
- What thoughts were running through my mind before, during, and after the situation?
- How was I behaving? [*name some specific behaviors*]

Now fill out the worksheet in as much detail as possible.

Situation: _____.

_____

_____

_____

Prior to Incident

People	Physiological sensations	Emotions	Cognitions/ thoughts	Behaviors
_____	_____	_____	_____	_____
_____	_____	_____	_____	_____
_____	_____	_____	_____	_____

During Incident

People	Physiological sensations	Emotions	Cognitions/ thoughts	Behaviors
_____	_____	_____	_____	_____
_____	_____	_____	_____	_____
_____	_____	_____	_____	_____

After Incident

People	Physiological sensations	Emotions	Cognitions/ thoughts	Behaviors
_____	_____	_____	_____	_____
_____	_____	_____	_____	_____
_____	_____	_____	_____	_____

WORKSHEET 13
Behavioral Triggers

What specific behaviors did you engage in before, during, and after you became suspicious? Were you very tired or stressed? Were you arguing? Were you waiting for someone? What did you do in response to your feelings and thoughts?

Before:

Behavior 1 _____.

Behavior 2 _____.

Behavior 3 _____.

During:

Behavior 1 _____.

Behavior 2 _____.

Behavior 3 _____.

After:

Behavior 1 _____.

Behavior 2 _____.

Behavior 3 _____.

Detail as much information regarding your behaviors as possible. Use the lines below.

_____

_____

_____

_____

_____

_____

_____

_____

_____

_____

WORKSHEET 14
Behavioral Triggers & Suggested Interventions

Scan the list you just made and identify which specific behaviors you wish to address.

Behavior 1 _____.

Behavior 2 _____.

Behavior 3 _____.

What can you do instead?

Stop

Take a moment to stop. If you are experiencing thoughts or feelings that make you question others' intentions, or if you feel as if someone is harming you, be sure to stop. In this way, you can give yourself extra time to examine the situation more fully and make an informed decision about your reaction rather than acting impulsively.

Monitor Yourself and Others

One way to determine if your reactions are appropriate to the situation at hand is to watch what others are doing. If other people are not yelling or are not suspicious of others around you, use this information to assist you in not becoming overly anxious or distressed. Remember, all people have the ability to detect danger. Use others as a way of seeing if the "coast is clear."

When I become suspicious I notice I am _____

_____

_____.

When I become suspicious I notice that others _____

_____

_____.

In the past when I was suspicious and realized I shouldn't have been, others were behaving

_____

_____

_____.

Message Chart

Communication is a three-step process. It begins with the *sender* of the message. This is the person trying to tell or show the other person something. Then there is the actual *message* itself. The message itself has the mission to reach the *receiver* of the information. When you are suspicious or scared, as the receiver, you have interpreted the sender and their message as frightening.

The Message Chart		
Sender	**Message**	**Receiver**
_____ .	_____ .	_____ .
_____ .	_____ .	_____ .
_____ .	_____ .	_____ .
_____ .	_____ .	_____ .
_____ .	_____ .	_____ .

What senders have the potential to send fearful messages?

_____

_____

_____ .

What messages particularly frighten you?

_____

_____

_____ .

As a receiver, utilize "I" statements to clarify the sender's message. When I am unclear about what a message means, I can use the statement, I _____. The exercise below further defines "I" statements.

Assert Yourself

If you have made a negative assumption, try to assert yourself to find out if you're making the right assumption. You can use "I" statements to let others know how you feel and thus test your perceptions. "I" statements originate from you. As we cannot begin to guess or assume what others are contemplating, one way of clarifying a situation that causes you distress is to assert yourself—to make a statement about how *you* are feeling or perceiving what is happening. In this way, you may prevent miscommunication with someone else and avoid uncomfortable feelings of suspicion. It also lets the other person clarify the situation. When you phrase the question as something that you are experiencing—without placing blame on the other—it allows the other person to reflect on what you are saying and feeling and to begin clear communication.

For example:

"I feel _____ [*sad, anxious, angry, scared*] right now. Can we take a moment to talk about this?"

I am feeling _____

I _____

_____ .

WORKSHEET 16
Situational Triggers

There may be times, individuals, events, and places that trigger your feelings of suspicion. Knowing which situations cause you difficulty can help you be prepared if a similar situation occurs; in particular you can be on alert for your alarms. You identified your four areas of warning signs in Worksheet 3: The Incident Chart. Now list the situations in which you have experienced feelings of suspiciousness. Does it seem to occur with one particular person? Do you feel more suspicious during times of stress? Do you note any patterns? Review Worksheet 1 if you need help identifying these situations.

1. _____

_____

_____.

2. _____

_____

_____.

3. _____

_____

_____.

4. _____

_____

_____.

5. _____

_____

_____.

6. _____

_____

_____.

WORKSHEET 17
Situational Triggers & Suggested Interventions

WORKSHEET 16 identifies those situations in which you have experienced feeling suspicious. If you are in a situation similar to or included in that list, the following interventions can help you avoid or manage suspicion.

Remove Yourself

Once you have identified potentially stressful situations, remember, you can choose to remove yourself from similar situations. For example, if you know that during arguments you tend to become overwhelmed and jump to conclusions about the motives of the other person, make a plan to discontinue the interaction or exit the situation.

When things get particularly difficult, I can _____

_____

_____

_____

_____

_____

_____

_____.

Try Something Different

Once you have identified those situations that cause suspicion, try a different behavior in similar situations. For example, if you find you are becoming suspicious with a particular individual, instead of becoming quiet or withdrawn, begin a conversation with a different individual.

Instead of _____ [*behavior*],

I can try _____

_____

_____

_____

_____

_____

_____.

Your therapist will help you complete this worksheet.

FREEMAN DIAGNOSTIC PROFILING SYSTEM
(© FREEMAN, 2003) REVISED EDITION

Date of Assessment: _____

Session#: _____ Evaluator: _____

Patient Name: _____ Patient#: _____ Location: _____

Birthdate: _____ Age: _____ Race: _____ Gender: _____ Birthorder: _____ Marital/Children: _____

Employment: _____ Education: _____ Disability: _____ Medication: _____

Physician: _____ Referral Question: _____

Instructions: Record the diagnosis including the code number. Briefly identify the criteria for the selected diagnosis. Working with the patient either directly as as part of the data gathering of the clinical interview, SCALE the SEVERITY of EACH CRITERION for the patient at the PRESENT TIME. Indicate the level of severity on the grid.

DIAGNOSIS (DSM/ICD) with Code:

Axis I: _____

Axis II: _____

Axis III: _____

SEVERITY OF SYMPTOMS / HIGH / MEDIUM / LOW grid, vertical axis 1–10, horizontal axis 0–12

DESCRIPTIVE CRITERIA

CRITERIA:

1 _____   7 _____

2 _____   8 _____

3 _____   9 _____

4 _____   10 _____

5 _____   11 _____

6 _____   12 _____

Do you believe that the above noted criteria are a reaonably accurate sample of the patient's behavior? **YES** or **NO**

If **NO**, please indicate why: _____

Are there any reasons to believe that this individual is an imminent danger to himself/herself or others? **YES** or **NO**

If **YES**, please indicate the danger: _____

(From Freeman, 1998.)

CHALLENGING WHAT YOU KNOW & DO: TAKING CONTROL

We all have times when we are frightened. Becoming frightened is an important survival function that alerts us to impending danger. However, for some of us, becoming scared and suspicious of others becomes a pattern. We might have learned it as child, perhaps as a result of some traumatic experience. In other words, our alarm systems are now turned up so high that they scan for danger where it doesn't exist. Keep in mind that there are times when we should be afraid. But there also are times when we experience a false alarm. Those are the times that you can work on. With practice, you can learn to question whether or not your fears or suspicions are the result of a real intruder or of a system that is turned up too high. You can then react appropriately.

CHAPTER 10 | Inside & Outside: Views of Yourself

As a sensitive individual exquisitely attuned to potential losses and rejection, at times of extreme stress you might feel almost as if you are watching yourself from a distance or are not completely in your body. These feelings result in a sensation of detachment, where you feel like you are in a "fog" or as if you're watching yourself interact, work, and exist amongst everyone else from a distance.

During these episodes, you may not have been able to function as well as you normally would. Normal tasks can become very difficult to complete; work might be nearly impossible to do. While these strange sensations are occurring, you might be fearful that you will never return to feeling "normal." This, for good reason, causes much fear and panic. However, these states are usually short-lasting. They generally occur when a threat of loss or rejection occurs in combination with extreme stress, and they subside when the threat passes.

As a child, you might have learned to detach or remove yourself as a means of coping with threats of abandonment. In a sense, you remove yourself from the situation by assuming a detached presence. As an adult, it may be difficult to address these odd feelings. Yet, no matter how different you might feel, or even how out of control you feel, you can effect a change for yourself. The important thing to remember is that by recognizing that this is a personal pattern, you are taking the first step toward learning how to predict, handle, and change these experiences. Your therapist may suggest a physical exam to ensure that not only the mind is being helped but also the body.

VIGNETTES

Vignette 1: Mary

Mary had gotten little sleep in the past two nights. Her constant arguments with her mother were exhausting, and now her mother was threatening to kick her out. She was so tired that she was dozing off at her desk. She meant to finish the director's report, but the computer screen in front of her seemed to be blending the letters together. Her supervisor, noticing that Mary had stopped typing for at least 30 minutes, stormed into her cubicle and began firing a series of questions at her: "Why aren't you finished yet? What's taking so long? What are you doing?" Her supervisor concluded, "This is a final warning!" Mary's heart was pounding faster and faster, and she felt sick. Then suddenly, it didn't matter. She felt herself slipping out of the conversation, out of the chair, and nearly out of the room. She saw her supervisor's finger wagging at her and saw her mouth moving, but she just couldn't for the life of her answer in any kind of organized way.

Finally her supervisor pounded her desk. This jerked her back to her senses which only make her feel lousy again.

Vignette 2: John

"I'm leaving John!" Suzie shouted. She was picking out items of clothing; her favorite ones at that; and throwing them into a large duffel bag. "I just can't take your drinking anymore or your incredible bad moods. I'm staying with Mom for a few days until this is sorted out." John watched, bewildered, as his wife continued to collect things to leave. He saw her moving, he saw her talking to him, he saw her hair flouncing about as she moved throughout their bedroom. He suddenly felt as if this whole scene wasn't real. It just didn't feel like it was happening. It seemed as if he was watching one of those Woody Allen movies where a couple is supposed to have some kind of sophisticated conversation or something. He couldn't speak; he couldn't move. He hopelessly and helplessly stood by, not really there, watching his wife leave him.

Review the Vignettes

Do either of these scenarios seem familiar to you? Do you sometimes feel as if you are detached? In both situations, the characters are under extreme amounts of stress, with threats of significant others either leaving or changing the relationship. Mary, frightened that her mother was going to kick her out, became overwhelmed by physical exhaustion and extreme stress at work. John, overwhelmed by the idea that his wife was truly leaving him, watched helplessly from a safe vantage point by remaining detached from the scene.

Note their warning signs. Both were tired and stressed. Both were trying to handle difficult situations related to abandonment by significant others. Both also felt strange sensations just before they became detached. Does this happen to you?

WHAT YOU WOULD LIKE TO CHANGE

First, discuss with your therapist whether this seems to be an area that is problematic for you. Do you relate to the vignettes? Does this behavior appear to occur in a pattern? Is it an area of your life over which you wish you had more control? If it does not seem pertinent, discuss with your therapist whether you need to continue to the assessment section.

SELF-MONITORING: HOW DO I KNOW WHAT MY PERCEPTIONS ARE?

By now you are very familiar with your internal alarm system. However, when you are put under extreme stress, feelings of detachment kick in to shut down your alarm system. This happens in an effort to save you from having to experience painful sensations and feelings. However, by detaching, you are not really addressing the very problem that is causing your detachment. It is a short-term solution. You no longer are in the room, so to speak, to challenge or question what is happening. By learning to read your sensors when you become extremely stressed or overwhelmed, you can begin to thwart your usual coping mechanism, detachment. The goal, therefore, is to find out if there are certain events or situations that trigger you, or if a particular combination of ingredients typically leads you to become detached.

THE WORKSHEETS

The following section includes several worksheets that address the current chapter topic. The worksheets are designed to help you learn more about yourself so that you can decide if there is anything you wish to change. Your therapist can help you use them.

WORKSHEET 1
The Assessment

Rate the severity of the following problems as you think they relate to you.

0 = none   1 = mild   2 = moderate   3 = severe   4 = extremely severe

1. You feel as if you have watched yourself from outside your body.   ___

2. You can easily tune others out when you are talking with them.   ___

3. When stressed, you sometimes feel as if you are in a dream.   ___

4. You have felt a lack of control of your body when stressed.   ___

5. You have experienced feeling like a robot or automaton.   ___

6. When arguing with a loved one, it almost seems as if you exist in a movie.   ___

7. Stressful situations or events seem unreal to you.   ___

8. If you are overtired, you sometimes don't feel attached or grounded to anything.   ___

9. Your friends and family describe you as "spacey."   ___

10. There are brief periods of time you can't account for or have an unclear memory of.   ___

Do any of these situations apply to you? Although we all sometimes feel "out of it," feelings of detachment are more patterned. You might have noticed that some of these behaviors occur when you are arguing with a significant other and/or when you are extremely stressed. Perhaps you feel as if these episodes are out of your control or that once they start, you have no means of stopping them. If, however, you can learn to identify the things and situations that trigger this type of reaction, you can begin to protect or pad yourself for future occurrences. As experiencing these episodes can be quite frightening, it is important that you remember that they usually are short-lasting and are not permanent. Additionally, there are things you can do to stop them if you begin to sense that they may recur.

WORKSHEET 2
The Assignment

Think of the last time you experienced a trancelike state or were detached from yourself. You might have felt outside of yourself or you might have felt numb. Perhaps it occurred when you were fighting with someone, breaking up with someone, or fearing that you had been left. Try to piece together the entire situation. Use the lines below to detail your experience. Be as specific as possible. You will compile your reactions in WORKSHEET 3: THE INCIDENT CHART.

_____

_____

_____

_____

_____

_____

_____

_____

_____

_____

_____

_____

_____

_____

_____

_____

_____

_____

_____

_____

_____

_____

_____

WORKSHEET 3
The Incident Chart*

This worksheet will help you begin uncovering the schema related to this characteristic. Think about the situation you described in WORKSHEET 2 and ask yourself the following:

- What was I physically experiencing before, during, and after the situation?
- What was I feeling?
- What thoughts were running through my mind before, during, and after the situation?
- How was I behaving? [*name some specific behaviors*]

Now fill out the worksheet in as much detail as possible.

Situation: _____

_____.

Prior to Incident

Physiological sensations	Emotions	Cognitions/ thoughts	Behaviors
_____ .	_____ .	_____ .	_____
_____ .	_____ .	_____ .	_____
_____ .	_____ .	_____ .	_____
_____ .	_____ .	_____ .	_____

During Incident

Physiological sensations	Emotions	Cognitions/ thoughts	Behaviors
_____ .	_____ .	_____ .	_____
_____ .	_____ .	_____ .	_____
_____ .	_____ .	_____ .	_____
_____ .	_____ .	_____ .	_____

After Incident

Physiological sensations	Emotions	Cognitions/ thoughts	Behaviors
_____ .	_____ .	_____ .	_____
_____ .	_____ .	_____ .	_____
_____ .	_____ .	_____ .	_____

*(Adapted from J. S. Beck, *Cognitive Therapy: Basics and Beyond.* Guilford Press, 1995©.)

WORKSHEET 4
The DTR*

This worksheet is designed to assist you in identifying your automatic thoughts. Noting your automatic thoughts can help you determine what underlying schemas or beliefs relate to particular events or situations. What are your automatic thoughts related to feeling detached or outside yourself? For example, when you begin to feel stressed, do you experience thoughts such as "I can't possibly handle this stress" or "I need to feel numb to face this stress"? Your therapist will help you with the rest.

Date/Time	Situation	Automatic thought	Emotion	Adaptive response	Outcome

*(Adapted from J. S. Beck, *Cognitive Therapy: Basics and Beyond*. Guilford Press, 1995©.)

WORKSHEET 5
Schemas

What are your rules or schemas related to becoming detached? Take a moment to write them down.

_____

_____

_____

_____

_____

_____

_____.

Choose any of the specific rules and fill in each of the columns. Indicate what the rule is, where (or whom) it comes from, what meaning it has for you, and how likely or easy it would be for you to change that rule. Once you have identified your particular schemas, how strong they are, and whether or not they can be changed, you can begin to create treatment goals.

Schema	Where it comes from	Meaning to me	Easy to change?

WORKSHEET 6
Treatment Goals

This worksheet asks you to identify your treatment goals, the symptoms that prevent you from obtaining your goals, the schemas that are associated with those goals, and the change that you are hoping for. Are you able to imagine yourself completing the goals? Complete this chart with the help of your therapist and prioritize the importance of each of these goals.

	Symptoms that prevent you from obtaining goal	Schema associated with goal	Hoped-for change	Realistic or unrealistic?	How outcome looks if goal is reached
Goal 1: **Highest priority**					
Goal 2: **High priority**					
Goal 3: **Moderate priority**					
Goal 4: **Low priority**					

The DPS

Your therapist will help you complete this worksheet.

FREEMAN DIAGNOSTIC PROFILING SYSTEM

(© FREEMAN, 2003) REVISED EDITION

Date of Assessment: _____

Session#: _____ Evaluator: _____

Patient Name: _____ Patient#: _____ Location: _____

Birthdate: _____ Age: _____ Race: _____ Gender: _____ Birthorder: _____ Marital/Children: _____

Employment: _____ Education: _____ Disability: _____ Medication: _____

Physician: _____ Referral Question: _____

Instructions: Record the diagnosis including the code number. Briefly identify the criteria for the selected diagnosis. Working with the patient either directly as as part of the data gathering of the clinical interview, SCALE the SEVERITY of EACH CRITERION for the patient at the PRESENT TIME. Indicate the level of severity on the grid.

DIAGNOSIS (DSM/ICD) with Code:

Axis I: _____

Axis II: _____

Axis III: _____

SEVERITY OF SYMPTOMS — DESCRIPTIVE CRITERIA

CRITERIA:

1 _____   7 _____

2 _____   8 _____

3 _____   9 _____

4 _____   10 _____

5 _____   11 _____

6 _____   12 _____

Do you believe that the above noted criteria are a reaonably accurate sample of the patient's behavior? **YES** or **NO**

If **NO**, please indicate why: _____

Are there any reasons to believe that this individual is an imminent danger to himself/herself or others? **YES** or **NO**

If **YES**, please indicate the danger: _____

(From Freeman, 1998.)

WORKSHEET 7
Physical Triggers

Physical sensations are clues to help you avoid future distressful situations. Your physical warning signs can be difficult to read if you are becoming detached. You might experience a numb sensation or an inability to sense things around you. What are your physical warning signs that you are becoming detached? For instance, you may recognize warning signs related to fear (racing heart) or anxiety (stomach or GI distress). Think of the experience you described in WORKSHEET 2: THE ASSIGNMENT. What were you physically experiencing before, during, and after you became detached? You might have felt some of the following:

- queasy stomach.
- sweating/clammy skin.
- racing heart.
- tension.
- GI distress.

Use the lines below to describe your physical sensations.

_____

_____

_____

_____

_____

_____

_____

_____

_____

_____

_____

_____

_____

_____

_____.

WORKSHEET 8
Physical Triggers & Suggested Interventions

Determining the exact physical symptoms of impending detachment will require careful self-monitoring. Once you have identified them, however, you can use three techniques to combat them: (1) take a moment to stop; (2) employ relaxation techniques; and (3) use relaxing imagery.

Stop

In WORKSHEET 4, you identified the thoughts directly related to your experience of feeling detached. For this exercise, identify the thoughts that seem to be creating or exacerbating uncomfortable physical reactions. Use the lines below to write down those thoughts.

_____

_____

_____

_____

_____

_____.

If you notice that your physical system responds in a particular way just before you begin to detach, take a moment to stop as soon as you feel that symptom.

As soon I feel _____ , I tend to become detached.

Relax

In WORKSHEET 3, you identified what specific physical symptoms occur when you becoming detached. If you know what physical symptoms are related to becoming detached, you can utilize relaxation techniques when you experience those symptoms. Relaxing directly contradicts arousal and helps prevent detaching.

You can do this by _____

_____

_____

_____

_____

_____.

Relaxing Imagery

Often detaching occurs when we are threatened, frightened, or overwhelmed with anxiety. If you note your physical alarms are becoming activated, combine stopping with relaxation techniques while imagining yourself in a safe place.

I feel safe imagining _____

_____

_____

_____.

I hear _____

_____

_____

_____.

I feel _____

_____

_____

_____.

I can see _____

_____

_____

_____.

I can smell _____

_____

_____

_____.

I can taste _____

_____

_____

_____.

My safe person who can join me here is _____

_____

_____

_____.

WORKSHEET 9
Emotional Triggers

How would you describe the emotions you had when you started to detach? Can you identify one particular emotion that is related? Perhaps you felt extreme despair, fear, or rage. You might have felt totally isolated or alone and panicked. Use WORKSHEETS 3 and 4 to identify some of the feelings you had when you started to detach. The might include some of the following:

- fear.
- anger.
- sadness.
- disgust.

What were you feeling emotionally? Write down what those feelings were like.

_____

_____

_____

_____

_____

_____

_____

_____

_____

_____

_____

_____

_____

_____

_____

_____

_____

WORKSHEET 10
Emotional Triggers & Suggested Interventions

The following exercises are designed to help you with your emotions. Sometimes emotions become so powerful that decisions are made "from the heart," without thinking. These exercises can help you understand your emotions and how they can impact your decisions.

Scale Back

As you are a very sensitive person, feelings of detachment can be both frightening and inappropriate. You might feel as if you have no control over your own body or emotions. Perhaps you learned to fear that you will randomly reexperience another trancelike state and lose all sense of control. If you are able to clearly identify the emotion you usually have before you detach, try scaling back to avoid further distress.

Pick one of the uncomfortable emotional responses you wish to address from WORKSHEET 9. On a scale of 1 to 10 (1 being least severe and 10 being most severe), rate the severity of the emotion you experienced when you began feeling detached.

 1   2   3   4   5   6   7   8   9   10

As you continue to have uncomfortable emotions related to detaching, try to scale back or "turn the oven down." You might want to combine scaling back with some relaxation techniques described in WORKSHEET 8 on physical triggers. Once you have turned yourself down, rate your emotions again.

 1   2   3   4   5   6   7   8   9   10

How did you do? Were you able to turn yourself down? You'll notice that with practice, turning down your own emotional temperature becomes easier and easier. Can you describe how you are feeling now?

_____

_____

_____

_____

_____

_____

_____

_____

_____

_____

_____

WORKSHEET 11
Cognitive/Automatic Thoughts

Your thoughts may be related to catastrophic outcomes or feeling unable to cope. Did you make statements to yourself that you had no control over things? You might have made statements about a significant other's leaving you. What thoughts were running through your mind before, during, and after you detached? Refer to WORKSHEET 4: THE DTR to help identify the specific thoughts related to this topic. Write your responses below.

_____

_____

_____

_____

_____

_____

_____

_____

_____

_____

_____

_____

_____

_____

_____

_____

_____

_____

_____

WORKSHEET 12
Cognitive/Automatic Thoughts & Suggested Interventions

Review WORKSHEETS 1 and 2 to determine when you typically tend to detach. Your cognitive interpretation of events might be activating your internal sensory system. You might be making conclusions or assumptions about significant others that include themes of abandonment, hopelessness, or low self-esteem. Perhaps you are making self-statements that you have no control. This may then lead you to detach as a means of protecting yourself.

Loss of control is experienced during a trancelike state. And when you feel out of control, you may lose the ability to assert yourself. The following techniques can be helpful in this regard.

Use WORKSHEET 15: THE EXPANDED INCIDENT CHART to detail your scenario. In addition to asking what your cognitions, emotions, physiological symptoms, and behaviors are, identify the people and situations that seem to trigger your trancelike states. What were your thoughts prior to detaching? Were you feeling left, hopelessness, or putting yourself down? Are your experiences a result of how you interpreted the situation? If you become overhwhelmed within the situation you might perceive that you are no longer in control and that your worst fears are being realized. Loss of control is experienced during a trancelike state. When one feels out of control, one loses the ability to assert oneself. You can feel so overwhelmed with emotion that you are unable to clearly express your fears, feelings, and assumptions. In sum, you might not be able to verify if what you are perceiving is real information or a product of your own filter system which has led to a patterned response to the situation.

WORKSHEET 15
The Expanded Incident Chart

Think about the situation you described in WORKSHEET 2: THE ASSIGNMENT and ask yourself the following:

- What was I physically experiencing before, during, and after the situation?
- What was I feeling?
- What thoughts were running through my mind before, during, and after the situation?
- How was I behaving? [*name some specific behaviors*]
- Is there a specific person or group associated with this situation?

Now fill out the worksheet in as much detail as possible.

Situation: _____

_____

_____

_____

_____

Prior to Incident

People	Physiological sensations	Emotions	Cognitions/ thoughts	Behaviors
_____ .	_____ .	_____ .	_____ .	_____ .
_____ .	_____ .	_____ .	_____ .	_____ .
_____ .	_____ .	_____ .	_____ .	_____ .

During Incident

People	Physiological sensations	Emotions	Cognitions/ thoughts	Behaviors
_____ .	_____ .	_____ .	_____ .	_____ .
_____ .	_____ .	_____ .	_____ .	_____ .
_____ .	_____ .	_____ .	_____ .	_____ .

After Incident

People	Physiological sensations	Emotions	Cognitions/ thoughts	Behaviors
_____ .	_____ .	_____ .	_____ .	_____ .
_____ .	_____ .	_____ .	_____ .	_____ .
_____ .	_____ .	_____ .	_____ .	_____ .

Challenge Catastrophic Thinking

Challenge both your thoughts of abandonment and lack of self-control. For example, if you are overwhelmed with distress and multiple stressors, do you have thoughts such as "I can't handle this" or "I want to feel numb"? Challenge these thoughts with "I can handle this" or "Not being numb will help me handle the situation."

The Catastrophic Thinking Chart		
Situation	Catastrophic thought	Noncatastrophic thought

Some additional suggestions are:

- Ask yourself "What if?" questions.
  Ask yourself, "What if this is true? What if it isn't?"

- Ask yourself "common-sense" questions.
  When you ask yourself "common-sense" questions such as "Could this really be happening?" or "Could I be reading this wrong?" you challenge your beliefs about what you may be perceiving or experiencing.

- Reflect on previous experiences.
  Consider whatever situation is making you feel uncomfortable. Have you been in a similar situation in the past? What was the result of that situation?

Ground Yourself

As soon as you have identified that a trigger has occurred, try to focus on something that grounds you or helps you feel in control. You might want to try to imagine someone or something in your life that is stable. For example, if you are experiencing great stress and begin to feel detached, imagine something heavy and comforting around you, like a large, warm blanket that won't let you float away.

Some other ways to ground yourself:

- Imagine wearing a heavy pair of boots that won't let you float away.
- Imagine a trusted family member holding onto you. [*use a picture to reinforce this*]
- Sit in a chair and allow all of your weight to sink into the chair.

When I am overwhelmed I can ground myself by _____
_____
_____
_____
_____

WORKSHEET 13
Behavioral Triggers

What specific behaviors did you engage in before, during, and after you detached? Were you very tired or stressed? Were you working or talking with someone? What did you do in response to your feelings and thoughts? Did you stare into space or stand frozen in one spot?

Before:

Behavior 1 _____.

Behavior 2 _____.

Behavior 3 _____.

During:

Behavior 1 _____.

Behavior 2 _____.

Behavior 3 _____.

After:

Behavior 1 _____.

Behavior 2 _____.

Behavior 3 _____.

Detail as much information regarding your behaviors as possible. Use the lines below.

_____

_____

_____

_____

_____

_____

_____

_____

_____

_____.

WORKSHEET 14
Behavioral Triggers & Suggested Interventions

Scan the list you just made and identify which specific behaviors you wish to address.

Behavior 1 _____.

Behavior 2 _____.

Behavior 3 _____.

What can you do instead?

Monitor Yourself and Others

When you feel that something frightening or stressful is occurring, watch others around you to determine if your reactions are on target. If others are not reacting in the same way you are, you might be misreading the situation. Everyone is equipped to detect danger. If no one around you seems concerned, the situation probably isn't dangerous.

When I have detached in the past I noticed that I _____

_____.

When I detach I notice that others _____

_____.

When I detached but was later reassured that nothing bad was happening, around me others were behaving

_____.

Identify a Friend

If your alarm system is activated and you know that you might be starting to detach, contact or call a friend whom you trust and feel safe with. This person can then help you ground yourself.

When I become overwhelmed I can call/contact _____

_____.

Identify an Anchor

In combination with the grounding exercise, identify an anchor that helps remind you of safety and feeling protected. An anchor can be a thought, a specific item that makes you feel safe, or a mental image of yourself doing something that reminds you of safety. Some examples of anchors are:

- Imagine holding a heavy object.
- Imagine feeling solid ground beneath their feet.
- Imagine laying on warm sand on a beachtowel.

My anchors are: _____

_____.

WORKSHEET 16
Situational Triggers

There are times, individuals, events, and places that trigger your feelings of detachment. Knowing which situations cause you difficulty can help you be prepared if a similar situation occurs; in particular, you can be on alert for your alarms. You identified your four areas of warning signs in WORKSHEET 3: THE INCIDENT CHART. Now list the situations in which you have experienced detachment. Was it only in relation to someone you care very much about? Was it worse when you were stressed? Do you note any patterns? Review WORKSHEET 1 if you need help identifying these situations.

1. _____

_____

_____ .

2. _____

_____

_____ .

3. _____

_____

_____ .

4. _____

_____

_____ .

5. _____

_____

_____ .

6. _____

_____

_____ .

WORKSHEET 17
Situational Triggers & Suggested Interventions

WORKSHEET 16 identifies those situations in which you have experienced feeling detached. If you are in a situation similar to or included in that list, the following interventions can help you avoid or manage feeling detached.

Remove Yourself

Not all stressful situations can be avoided, however you might be able to identify themes of situations that trigger trancelike states and choose to either remove yourself, or structure the situation so that you feel more in control. For example, conflict-laden family gatherings usually produce extreme levels of stress. If the situation is unavoidable, there can be ways to manage it, such as limiting the duration of your visit.

When things get particularly difficult, I can _____

_____

_____

_____

_____

_____

_____ .

Try Something Different

If you notice that your alarm systems have been activated, try to change your pattern of usual reactions. If you experience extreme anxiety symptoms just before detaching, can you use that energy to take a walk? Or if you know that when you argue with someone you become numb or detached, can you instead try to call a friend or complete an activity you've wanted to finish?

Instead of _____ [*behavior*],

I can try _____

_____

_____

_____

_____

_____

_____ .

The DPS

Your therapist will help you complete this worksheet.

Date of Assessment: _____

FREEMAN DIAGNOSTIC PROFILING SYSTEM
(© FREEMAN, 2003) REVISED EDITION

Session#: _____ Evaluator: _____

Patient Name: _____ Patient#: _____ Location: _____

Birthdate: _____ Age: _____ Race: _____ Gender: _____ Birthorder: _____ Marital/Children: _____

Employment: _____ Education: _____ Disability: _____ Medication: _____

Physician: _____ Referral Question: _____

Instructions: Record the diagnosis including the code number. Briefly identify the criteria for the selected diagnosis. Working with the patient either directly as as part of the data gathering of the clinical interview, SCALE the SEVERITY of EACH CRITERION for the patient at the PRESENT TIME. Indicate the level of severity on the grid.

DIAGNOSIS (DSM/ICD) with Code:

Axis I: _____

Axis II: _____

Axis III: _____

SEVERITY OF SYMPTOMS — HIGH / MEDIUM / LOW (vertical axis 1–10)

DESCRIPTIVE CRITERIA (horizontal axis 0–12)

CRITERIA:

1 _____   7 _____

2 _____   8 _____

3 _____   9 _____

4 _____   10 _____

5 _____   11 _____

6 _____   12 _____

Do you believe that the above noted criteria are a reaonably accurate sample of the patient's behavior? **YES** or **NO**

If **NO**, please indicate why: _____

Are there any reasons to believe that this individual is an imminent danger to himself/herself or others? **YES** or **NO**

If **YES**, please indicate the danger: _____

(From Freeman, 1998.)

CHALLENGING WHAT YOU KNOW & DO: TAKING CONTROL

Feeling as if you are floating away, detached, or outside of yourself can be a frightening experience. We sometimes do it as a form of relaxation, such as daydreaming or allowing our thoughts to wander. Sometimes, however, it becomes a means of dealing with very stressful or overwhelming situations. Perhaps you learned at a very young age to manage stressful situations by going "outside of yourself." If you tend to detach when things are particularly tough, you might actually be limiting your options regarding how you want to react. In other words, if you are detached, you probably won't be able to think of all the options you have to deal with the situation. By taking control and learning when and how you detach, you can plan for any recurrences of these feelings. Once your alarm system has let you know you are facing a situation that might spark detached feelings, you can enact your grounding techniques and focus on the problem at hand. Once focused, you can decide exactly how you want to handle it; either by facing the situation now or by giving yourself some time to work things out.

Wrapping Up:
Taking Control of
Borderline Personality Disorder

Your personality is your unique and stable way of viewing yourself, your world, and your interactions with the world. It includes behaviors, feelings, thoughts, and interactions and reactions that tend to occur in the same way across time. The key is understanding that personality is not one specific trait but rather a pattern of physical responses, emotions, thoughts, and behaviors. Various traits and aspects of ourselves interact with one another in patterns that we learned as young children and young adults.

Understanding yourself and your patterns is dependent upon your ability to self-monitor, track your automatic thoughts, and identify your learned belief systems or schemas. It is this understanding of your physical, emotional, cognitive, and behavioral patterns and schemas, as well as your understanding of which situations trigger your patterned responses, that can empower you to change the responses you don't like and enhance the aspects of yourself that you do like. (For example, you may decide to change your tendency to lose your cool in arguments, but still let yourself become emotional when you watch a sad movie or read a dramatic

novel.) Additionally, in the process of deciding what level of change you wish to enact, you also will be growing and learning more about yourself.

Self-knowledge is power. By getting to know yourself and learning to predict how you might react in particular situations, you give yourself a wealth of choices and potential to try new paths. We all have the potential to continue learning, growing, and adapting. We crave knowledge about what will make us happy or satisfy our needs. We can learn ways of getting our needs met without feeling upset or out of control. If you identify with many BPD patterns, you might have felt a painful inconsistency in your life. Inconsistency often halts forward momentum or prevents you from accessing things you want or need. However, by learning about your patterns, you have, in effect, begun the process of taking control.

By continually monitoring your warning signs, you will begin to see the actual differences in each and every situation and realize that each situation offers you the opportunity for something new, healthy, and even exciting.

References

American Psychiatric Association (2000). *Diagnostic and statistical manual of mental disorders (4th ed. text revision)*. Washington, DC: Author.

Beck, A. (1986). Hopelessness as a predictor of eventual suicide. *Annals of the New York Academy of Science, 487*, 90–96.

Beck, A., & Emery, G. (1979). *Cognitive therapy of anxiety and phobic disorders*. Philadelphia: Center for Cognitive Therapy.

Beck, J. (1995). *Cognitive therapy: Basics and beyond*. New York: Guilford Press.

Bernstein, D., & Borkovec, T. (1976). *Progressive relaxation training: A manual for the helping professionals*. Champaign, IL.: Research Press.

Freeman, A. (1998). *The Diagnostic Profiling System*. Unpublished manuscript.

Freeman, A., Pretzer, J., Fleming, B., & Simon, K. (1990). *Clinical applications of cognitive therapy*. New York: Plenum Press.

Jacobson, E. (1962). *You must relax*. New York: McGraw-Hill.

Layden, M., Newman, C., Freeman, A., & Morse, S. (1993). *Cognitive therapy of borderline personality disorder*. Boston: Allyn & Bacon.

Pretzer, J. (1990). Borderline personality disorder. In A. Beck, A. Freeman, & Associates (Eds.), *Cognitive therapy for personality disorders* (pp. 176–207). New York: Guilford Press.

Tracy Fields. Swarthmore PA

Gina M. Fusco, Psy.D. is a licensed psychologist and is a System of Care Clinical Director for Alternative Behavioral Services, a comprehensive behavioral healthcare program for high-risk adolescents. She has authored and coauthored chapters on the treatment of crisis-prone patients, crisis intervention, and personality disorders. She lectures at the Philadelphia College of Osteopathic Medicine and Chestnut Hill College in Philadelphia.

Courtesy of PCOM

Arthur Freeman, Ed.D., is Professor and Chair of the Department of Psychology at the Philadelphia College of Osteopathic Medicine and is on the core faculty of the Adler School of Professional Psychology. In addition to 50 book chapters, reviews, and journal articles, he has published thirty professional books and two popular books, *Woulda, Coulda, Shoulda: Overcoming Mistakes and Missed Opportunities* and *The Ten Dumbest Mistakes Smart People Make, and How to Overcome Them*.